KU-619-110

CONTENTS

SYMBOLS KEY

The following is a key to the symbols used throughout this book:

i	information office	✈	airport	🍴	restaurant
🚌	bus stop	↘	tip	☕	café
✉	post office	🛍	shopping	☕	fine dining

❶ telephone   **❶** fax   **e** email   **w** website address

a address   **🕐** opening times   **❶** important

E£ budget price   E£users mid-range price   E£££ most expensive

★ specialist interest   ★★ see if passing   ★★★ top attraction

Getting to know Egypt

The Red Sea resorts are just a four-hour flight – and millennia apart – from the capitals of Europe. Packed with history, charm and fantastic diving opportunities, they have become key winter destinations for sun-seekers from across Britain and beyond. So, down a bottle of Saqqara beer, plunge into warm, turquoise waters and enjoy a meal of *ta'amiya* and *fuul*, because your trip to the cradle of civilization is about to begin.

GEOGRAPHY

Resorts on the Red Sea are divided into two geographical regions: the Sinai peninsula, and the mainland coast, running approximately 1000 km (620 miles) from Zafarana to the Sudanese border (see map on pages 6–7).

The chief resort on the Sinai peninsula is Sharm el-Sheikh, although Dahab and Nuweiba attract holidaymakers too. On the mainland coast, Hurghada is the capital of pleasure, with Marsa Alam and El Gouna as popular contenders.

In the Sinai interior, the topography becomes quite mountainous. It is among these great rocks that the ancient stories involving Moses fleeing away from the Pharaoh through the desert were set. Mount Sinai, for which the peninsula is named, is widely believed to be the location where Moses received the Ten Commandments.

A few kilometres away from the mainland coast are the wilds of the Eastern Desert. This stretch of land is extremely unforgiving, and dotted with rock paintings left by the nomads of the past.

TRADITIONS & COMMUNITIES

Most Egyptians living in resort towns rely on tourism for their income. Many have moved from other communities in the Nile Valley, drawn by the booming economy. As such, very few can claim to be locals, with the exception of the Bedouins. In the face of development, Bedouins are finding that their traditional lands are being taken over. They are mistrusted by Egyptians who feel that they have stronger links with fellow tribal members outside of the country. Both communities, Egyptians and Bedouins alike, are extremely friendly and welcoming. Get to know them and you will find that you will make friends fast.

LIFESTYLE

You might think that a trip to Egypt means no alcohol and that everything closes down on Friday evenings. This is certainly not the case. Egyptian people know the value of money and want tourists to enjoy themselves. Those working in the tourist industry go out of their way to make visitors feel comfortable. It is advisable, however, to keep local etiquette in mind and avoid wearing revealing bathing suits or skimpy clothing on public beaches or near mosques. Respect the Egyptians and in return a friendly smile will greet you on every street corner.

● *The Nile is one of the many excursions available from the Red Sea resorts*

ISRAEL

JORDAN

AIN SUKHNA

Wilderness of the
Wanderings

TABA

PHARAOH'S
ISLAND

ZA'FARANA

GULF
OF
SUEZ

SINAI

⑨

MONASTERY
OF ST
ANTHONY

TURQUOISE MINES

⑩

⑧

⑥

MONASTERY
OF ST PAUL

⑦

Nuweiba

ST CATHERINE'S
MONASTERY

①

Dahab

SAUDI ARABIA

Ras Gharib

③

Eastern
Desert

Nabq

④

Na'ame Bay

SHARM
EL-SHEIKH

②

EL GOUNA

El Fanadir

RAS MOHAMED

Umm Gamar

HURGHADA

Sha'ab Ruhr Umm Gamar
Careless Reef

Mons
Porphyritis

Giftun
Island

Abu Ramada
Gota Abu Ramada

Mons
Claudianus

Abu Hashish

PORT
SAFAGA

RED SEA

QENA

DIVE SITES

EL-QUESIR

① BLUE HOLE, THE CANYON
    & RAS ABU GALLUM

QUS

② RAS UMM SID, THE TOWER,
    AMPHORAS & TURTLE BAY

MARSA GALEB

LUXOR

③ SHARK BAY

River Nile

Wadi Mineh

④ TIRAN ISLAND
    PROTECTED AREA

⑤ DOLPHIN HOUSE

EDFU

Wadi Barramiyah

TREK SITES

MARSA ALAM

⑥ AIN AL-FURTEGA

KOM
OMBO

⑤

WADI GIMAL

⑦ AIN KHUDRA
    OASIS

N

ASWAN

⑧ AIN UMM AHMED

TOMB OF
SHEIKH EL-SHAZLI

⑨ COLOURED
    CANYON

0   150 km

⑩ WADI HUWEIYIT

0   100 miles

BERENICE

Eastern
Desert

Lake Nasser

SHALATEEN

SUDAN

The best of the Red Sea

EARLY CIVILIZATIONS

Egypt is widely recognized as the cradle of Western civilization. While the most important historic cities and sights are located within the Nile Valley, evidence of occupation along the coastline in the form of excavated temples and rock paintings is worthy of exploration.

- The coral reefs of Ras Mohamed showcase the glorious fish and coral that draw divers from around the world (page 81).
- St Catherine's Monastery (page 82) is a UNESCO World Heritage Site and an important place of pilgrimage for Coptic Christians.
- Camel safaris provide an insight into the harsh conditions of the Sinai or Eastern Desert. Travel with Bedouins for a truly memorable experience.
- Combine relaxation with a journey back through time to Cairo, Luxor or Aswan in a two-centre holiday (see Excursions, page 86 onwards).

⬤ Boat trips take visitors to the coral reefs

SHARM EL-SHEIKH

The capital of pleasure on the Sinai peninsula, Sharm el-Sheikh (see page 56) is a fascinating resort packed with luxurious hotels and excellent dive centres. The resort draws thousands of visitors every year, attracted to its glorious sunshine by day and vibrant nightlife. Explore the shopping at the central *souq* (market), take a day-trip to the nearby Nabq Mangrove Forest or enjoy swimming, snorkelling or diving in the Red Sea – the choice is yours. Restaurants offer almost every form of cuisine imaginable from Italian to Indonesian and the atmosphere is one of a Mediterranean resort with a Middle Eastern twist.

HURGHADA

This resort on the mainland coast (see page 72) is one of the most popular Egypt has to offer, loved by thousands of cosmopolitan locals and well-heeled Europeans every year. Definitely the nightlife capital of the resort community, it's a place for diving by day and dancing till dawn. Owing to its proximity to Luxor, it makes an ideal location for a two-centre holiday and is often chosen by visitors looking to experience a bit of history combined with a relaxing holiday.

MARSA ALAM

Further south down Egypt's mainland coast, Marsa Alam (see page 34) is remote yet well-endowed with facilities, and is rapidly becoming known as a great choice for those looking for a bit of peace and quiet – mobile phones are still a rarity here. Only recently developed as a tourist hotspot, it's perfect for active holidaymakers eager to explore the rocky interior of the Eastern Desert.

RESORTS
Red Sea coast

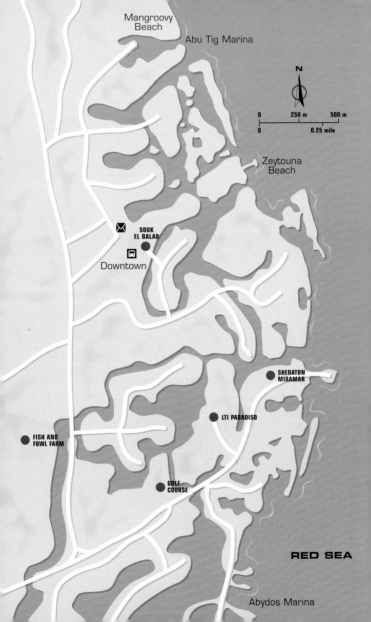

El Gouna
purpose-built for pleasure

This massive resort town is located 22 km (14 miles) north of Hurghada on a chain of islands linked by a series of bridges and canals. It has a visually stunning location set off by the contrast between the red sand of the desert and the turquoise lagoons which are dotted throughout the region. The amenities of the ultra-modern Abu Tig Marina, which was designed by Italian architect Alfredo Freda, is in complete contrast to the traditional feel of the town centre, Kafr El Gouna, with its vibrant bars, restaurants, shops and discos. Don't be fooled by the 'old' feel of the market square, though – everything here was actually built from scratch just 10 years ago.

A CITY ON THE SEA

The entire town of El Gouna was purpose-built for the tourist trade, and covers an incredible 17,000 sq km (6,564 sq miles). Over 10,000 people work on site in order to maintain an around-the-clock service in the hotels, two shopping centres, a hospital, four power plants, factories and an international airport. Fifteen resorts, ranging from three- to five-star, call El Gouna home, and there are more in the pipeline.

In order to keep a 'mini-city' on this scale in operation, investors have built a brewery that makes Saqqara and Löwenbrau beer, a cheese factory making mozzarella to supply the numerous pizzerias, as well as a decompression chamber for the diving community, and a winery.

THINGS TO SEE & DO

Pass the days at El Gouna by booking a dive through the dive centres found at the Sheraton Miramar, Three Corners Rihana Inn or LTI Paradisio Beach and Golf Hotel. If going underwater doesn't appeal, you will have plenty of other options.

Horse-riding, go-karting, tennis and squash are all available in the resort. For true thrill-seekers, there is even an operator who can teach you how to fly (or just ride in) a microlight plane.

🔺 *El Gouna*

SHOPPING

El Gouna's **Souk el Balad** is built to resemble a traditional
market and the place to go if you are looking for souvenirs.
Prices will be higher than average as all items are aimed towards
a tourist trade. If you are going to another resort in Egypt on a
twin-centre package, you may want to leave your shopping until
you reach your other destination.

Most visitors wind up in the main shopping centre at the end of an action-packed day. Here, holidaymakers will find numerous restaurants and bars, cafés, an open-air cinema, a school, museum, travel agencies where you can book onward passage, banks, an aquarium, a post office and nightclubs.

BEACHES

The man-made beaches of El Gouna, some only accessible by boat, are ideal for relaxation and there are numerous dive sites where you can see the splendour of the coral reefs. Because the entire town is dedicated to tourism and the beaches are only frequented by Egypt's upper classes, Western travellers will encounter far less hassle if they decide to take a stroll across the sand in their bathing costumes. Women in particular, will notice a distinct reduction in the number of stares compared to other resorts in the country.

Hotels own almost every inch of El Gouna's coast, so most of the beaches are private. If you do want to experience a different stretch of beach from the grains of sand that your hotel is situated on, you will have to pay a fee. The price can vary, but it is usually about E£20.

TIPS ON TRAVEL ARRANGEMENTS

Egypt's upper classes flock to El Gouna at every opportunity, mixing comfortably with the Western visitors who arrive primarily as part of a package tour. If you are considering a visit as an independent traveller, you would be well advised to think again as hotel rates offered to independent travellers are far more expensive than the heavily discounted rates included in a package, especially if you book well in advance.

Most people who visit El Gouna don't venture very far from their hotel and find plenty to occupy them in the town. However, there are bus services serving the coastal resorts of Hurghada and Safaga if you wish to travel further south.

◀ *Hurghada Mosque*

Hurghada
Egypt's 24-hour resort

In little over two decades, the town of Hurghada has been transformed from an overlooked fishing village into a booming resort which boasts a population of over 50,000. More than 100 hotels and resorts have been built since the mid-1980s, catering to an assortment of tourists ranging from no-star backpackers to five-star hedonists.

Tourism is what Hurghada is now about, accounting for more than 95 per cent of the local economy. However, the bid to boost the town coffers has come at a price. The once pristine waters are no longer as clean as they used to be, the coral reefs close to the coast that formerly beckoned divers with their beauty have been almost destroyed, and public beaches fail to inspire. Western women who attempt to sunbathe on a public beach will encounter uncomfortable hassling from local men.

THE BIG DRAW

Despite uncontrolled development, Hurghada is Egypt's most popular resort area because its range of facilities is unparalleled elsewhere in the country. It also has a well-developed network of dive centres that are especially good for beginners and a sense of authenticity that is lacking in other centres that opted to build Western-style resorts with European architecture. Hurghada offers a mix of styles and caters to all budgets.

A RUSSIAN REVOLUTION

Hurghada's tourist industry truly boomed from 1994 with the arrival of Russian holidaymakers. Faced with declining numbers of tourists, Hurghada's residents pulled out all the stops to welcome them. Today, the welcome mat is no less red than it used to be, and you still see *borsht* on restaurant menus to entice the Russian market. ❶ Try to plan your trip to avoid Russian holiday dates when prices are artificially inflated.

ORIENTATION

Hurghada has three main areas, all of which you are bound to visit at some point during your holiday.

Ad-Dahar (see map on page 23)

Ad-Dahar is the workaday, commercial centre where almost all of the budget accommodation can be found. It's in the northern end of town at the end of a long stretch of resorts that crowd the neighbourhood. Many of the buildings remain unfinished and are on unpaved streets.

Sigala (see map on page 25)

This is the fastest-growing part of the town. Separated from Ad-Dahar by a mountain, Gebel Ad-Dahar, it is packed with resorts that vie for a slice of sea frontage. Back from the beach are two- and three-star properties that are less lucky in their location. The main street is Sharia Sheraton, named after the resort that brought success to Sigala. Here you'll find most of the best restaurants and a lively crowd, day or night. If you plan to travel on to Sharm el-Sheikh or Dubai, ferries depart from the main passenger port.

The resort strip

South of Sigala, a road winds along the coast through the resort strip, and this is where all the five-star properties are located. Some 15 km (9 miles) south of Ad-Dahar, the road meets another, a few kilometres inland. This road marks the beginning of Hurghada's major development of new resorts which are in various stages of completion and stretch as far as Safaga. If you're looking for a change of pace, this road continues to Makadi Bay and Soma Bay – two up-and-coming luxury destinations.

THINGS TO SEE & DO

Aquarium ★

You may recognize some of the Red Sea fish and other marine creatures here. Tanks are labelled in English, so it is a good place for children, although some of the tanks (and specimens) look a little worse for wear. ⓐ Corniche, Ad-Dahar ⓣ 065 54 85 57 ⓛ Sat–Thur 09.00–22.00; Fri 09.00–noon and 13.00–22.00 ⓘ Admission charge

Sindbad Submarine ★

Take your aquatic adventure a step further! Tours by submarine dive to 22 m (72 ft), designed mostly as a photo opportunity. The trip takes two hours, half of it spent getting to and from the dive site. Once submerged, a diver swims along the side trailing bait to attract fish. ⓐ Bookings can be made at the Sindbad Hotel ⓣ 065 44 46 88 ⓘ Admission charge

Aquascope ★

A two-hour trip underwater in a bizarre contraption that looks like something from a sci-fi movie. Maximum 10 people per tour. ⓐ Departures from the Royal Palace Hotel ⓣ 065 44 49 06 ⓘ Admission charge

Beaches ★

Sigala's public beach has finally been cleaned up, but it is still quite stark and surrounded by development. Stick to private beaches for sunbathing, and go to the public beach later when you can rent a chair and watch the sun set – preferably sipping cocktails at Papas Beach Club or the Chill Bar.

Diving ⋆

Unlike Sharm el-Sheikh where diving operators are all generally acknowledged to offer top-quality experiences, some of Hurghada's are frankly dodgy and best avoided. Your life may even depend on it! ❶ Always check that your instructor is qualified with valid ID and insurance. Photocopies will not do.

Diving is what put Hurghada on the map but, owing to decades of tourism, much of the coral is destroyed. It is important to choose an operator who is aware of the environment to ensure that the coral you are paying to see remains healthy. Giftun Island, once the location divers dreamed of, has suffered badly and now needs drastic conservation.

You can do your bit towards the environment (and your personal health and safety) by selecting a dive centre that belongs to HEPCA (Hurghada Environmental Protection and Conservation Association), an organization that is attempting to address environmental issues by installing mooring buoys. For a full list of member centres, contact HEPCA on ❶ 065 44 66 74.

Costs and packages A typical four- or five-day PADI open-water course from a reputable diving centre should cost between £160 and £200 (US$280–350), including the certificate. A two-day advanced course will be from £110–145 (US$190–250). Beginners will have added costs in the form of an introductory lecture and two supervised dives. Expect to pay no more than £25–35 (US$45–60) extra. Scuba equipment should be included in the package price. For qualified divers, a day of boat diving averages out at £25–35 (US$45–60) and should include a minimum of two dives.

Liveaboards Living on board while diving, though more cost-effective for those who want to spend the bulk of their holiday diving, are tricky to arrange once you arrive in resort. It takes a minimum of six people to convince a captain to ship out. Book in advance to avoid disappointment. If you do get a liveaboard, check your boat has a radio, lifejackets, oxygen and a first-aid kit.

Diving excursions

There are dozens of dive sites within a day's journey from Hurghada. Some of the better ones include:

Abu Hashish Cave This cave is notable mostly for having once been used by drug smugglers.

Abu Ramada Just off Giftun Island, this dive site is OK if you are looking for fish but far more interesting if you prefer coral. There are three coral blocks here dripping with eye-poppingly bright soft corals.

Gota Abu Ramada A great spot to view spotted gropers, bannerfish and sweetlips. Keep an eye out for standing ergs (dune field) and 1500-year-old stony corals.

Careless Reef Accessible only in calm weather, but definitely worth any wait. See whitetip sharks and moray eels fight and mate around this plateau. It has an inspiring drop-off and Eden-like gardens of table and soft corals.

Samadai Reef ('Dolphin House') This horseshoe-shaped reef is better for snorkellers, but as the area is used by dolphins as a nursery it is well worth the trip. Buoys are installed to ensure no boats get in and disturb the newborns.

El-Fanadir Delightful reef slope featuring large table corals. One of the easiest sites to access from Hurghada.

Umm Gamar Island Drift divers will love this collection of caves and sheer walls. Allow yourself to glide along through the cave and you may find yourself caught up in a shoal of thousands of fish.

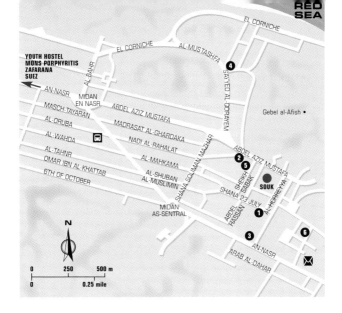

RESTAURANTS (AD-DAHAR, see map above)

🍴 **Pharaoh's Restaurant** E£ ❶ Tasty Egyptian food. The meat stew (*kebab hala*) comes highly recommended. ❷ Around the corner from the Red Sea Restaurant near Sharia An-Nasr ☎ 065 54 63 06 💰 Cash only

🍴 **Pizza Tarboush** E£ ❷ Shop in the *souq* and then drop into this busy pizza parlour serving up decent pizza with a variety of toppings. ❸ Sharia Abdel Aziz Mustafa ☎ 065 54 84 56 💰 Cash only

🍴 **Red Sea Restaurant** E££ ❸ When a package tourist decides to go off-resort, this is the place they head for. Seafood dishes are recommended. ❷ Sharia An-Nasr ☎ 065 54 77 04 💰 Cards accepted

🍴 **Lo Scarabeo** E££ ❹ Good selection of pizzas and pasta. Vegetarians will be thrilled to know that salads are what this place is known for. The portions of greenery are absolutely huge. That and the oregano-dusted bread. ❸ Sharia Sayyed al-Qorayem ☎ 012 36 46 927 💰 Cash only

Young Kang E£ **⑤** Surprisingly tasty Chinese–Korean eatery. The place is tiny, but everyone manages to make do in the confined space. Basics like fried rice and sweet-and-sour pork are your best options. Beer is also served. ⓐ Sharia Sheikh Sabak ⓣ 012 42 29 327 ⓘ Cash only

Zeko E£ **⑥** Grilled chicken, plain and simple. Enjoy it with rice and/or salad. That's the only decision you'll need to make here. ⓐ Sharia An-Nasr ⓘ Cash only

RESTAURANTS (SIGALA, see map on page 25)

Abu Khadega E£ **①** If you want to try basic Egyptian workers' grub, then this is the place to do it. Go for the excellent *kofte* and the chance to mix with locals. Good if you're on a tight budget. ⓐ Sharia Sheraton ⓣ 065 44 37 68 ⓘ Cash only

Bierkeller E£ **②** On a budget and sick of *fuul*? Head for Bierkeller. Hearty German food is dished up to the masses along with beer at this bar/restaurant. The food isn't much to write home about, but it will certainly fill you up. ⓐ Iberotel Arabella ⓣ 065 54 50 86 ⓘ Cards accepted

Bordiehn's E£production **③** Divine international dishes with a sense of creativity that go beyond most other menus in town. Ingredients are fresh (you can even try camel meat!) even if the atmosphere is a bit lacking. ⓐ Iberotel Arabella ⓣ 065 54 50 88 ⓘ Cards accepted

Bulls Steakhouse E££ **④** Missing meat? Look no further; the Bulls menu is a temple for carnivores. Chinese dishes, if less successful, are also on offer. ⓐ Resort Strip ⓣ 065 44 44 14 ⓘ Cards accepted

Da Nanni E£££ **⑤** The best pizza in town as made by the Italian couple who own the joint. ⓐ Resort Strip ⓣ 065 44 37 43 ⓘ Cards accepted

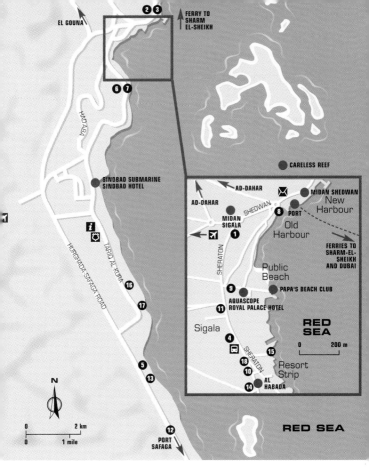

EL GOUNA

❷ ❸

❻ ❼

SINDBAD SUBMARINE
SINDBAD HOTEL

HADABA

CARELESS REEF

AD-DAHAR

AD-DAHAR

MIDAN SHEDWAN

MIDAN SIGALA ❶

SHEDWAN

❽ PORT

New Harbour

Old Harbour

FERRIES TO SHARM-EL-SHEIKH AND DUBAI

SHERATON

Public Beach

HURGHADA-SAFAGA ROAD

TARIQ AL-KURA

❻

❼

❾

PAPA'S BEACH CLUB

AQUASCOPE
ROYAL PALACE HOTEL

❶❶

Sigala

❹

SHERATON

RED SEA

0   200 m

❺

❶❸

N

❶❺

❶❽

❶❷

❶❹ AL HABADA

Resort Strip

0   2 km
0   1 mile

❶❷ PORT SAFAGA

RED SEA

El-Arabi E£ ❻ Local favourite known for its 'Oriental' food. Dishes are good-value. ❸ Sharia Sheraton, opposite the Seagull Hotel ❶ Cash only

Felfela E£££ ❼ Classic Egyptian cuisine in this branch of the popular Cairo-based chain. As the eatery sits on a rise, the views

25

⬥ *Relaxing at Hurghada*

of the sea are superb. Vegetarians are well-catered for. ❸ Sharia Sheraton, between the Holiday Inn and Sheraton ☎ 065 44 24 10 ❶ Cash only

🍴 **Joker** E££ ❽ Great seafood restaurant with excellent calamari. Portion sizes are generous, so it's worth working up an appetite. ❸ Near the police station in Sigala Square ☎ 065 54 31 46 ❶ Cash only

☕ **Omar Inn** E£ ❾ Small coffee-shop that offers takeaway snacks and pizzas for those on the go. ❸ Opposite the Golf Hotel ☎ 065 44 61 66 ❶ Cash only

🍴 **Rossi's** E£££ ❿ Italian dishes, especially good for crispy pizza; the pasta is hit or miss. Stick with the basics and you'll do fine. ❸ Sharia Sheraton opposite the now-defunct Aquafun waterpark. ☎ 065 44 60 12 ❶ Cash only

🔷 **Samos Restaurant** E£££ ⓫ If you fancy a meal of moussaka or savour a souvlaki, then Samos should fit the bill. ❸ Sharia Sheraton ☎ 012 23 38 027 ❶ Cards accepted

NIGHTLIFE

Alf Layla wa Layla ⓬ If you like your entertainment to be kitsch with a capital 'K', then this is for you. Described as a 'belly-dancing extravaganza', a brightly coloured show features Russian bellydancers swaying their way across a stage festooned with lights, dazzle and glitz. Not the place for those looking for an authentic introduction to this Middle Eastern dance form. ⓐ Safaga Road ⓣ 065 44 65 71 ⓘ Cards accepted

Black Out Disco ⓭ Incredibly popular Ibiza-style dance club with occasional foam parties. ⓐ Ali-Baba Palace, Resort Strip ⓣ 012 22 17 734 ⓘ Cash only

Calypso ⓮ Purpose-built bunker known more for its crowds of female Russian tourists than any hip resident DJs. The international cultural show is best avoided. ⓐ Sharia Al-Hadaba ⓣ 012 24 62 077 ⓘ Cards accepted

The Chill ⓯ Popular beach bar much favoured by the diving crowd and foreign residents. Every night sees a different style of music played, with dancing on weekends. Parties kick off after 23.00 and on nights with a full moon. Foreign DJs occasionally guest. ⓐ Sharia Sheraton, opposite the Roma Hotel ⓘ Cash only

The Dome ⓰ This club dedicated to dance has the best floor in town, but is limited to mixed-sex couples only. If the music tires, pass the time in the hotel's casino – the only one in town. Smart casual dress is required and guards may check your passport at the door. ⓐ Inter-Continental Hotel ⓣ 065 46 59 11 ⓘ Cards accepted

Hilton ⓱ Live music brings punters in six nights a week. And on the seventh night (Sunday), the Hilton created karaoke. Thursday night offers a free food and beer special that keeps divers coming in for more. ⓐ Hilton Resort, Resort Strip ⓣ 065 54 97 39 ⓘ Cards accepted

Papas Bar ⓲ Dutch-run drinking spot that is favoured by the diving crowd. ⓐ Sharia Sheraton, next to Rossi's ⓣ 010 51 29 051 ⓘ Cash only

Soma Bay
a putter's paradise

Soma Bay owes its place on Egypt's resort map to the massive five-star Sheraton resort, designed to reflect the art and architecture of ancient Egypt. Without it this sandy strip would be just another dot on the map.

Soma Bay is seen as the high-end hotspot of the region. Located 60 km (37 miles) south of Hurghada, it's a top-notch hideaway that caters especially well for golfers seduced by the impressive 18-hole championship **Cascades** golf course, fine sand beaches, magnificent coral reef and mountain backdrop. Facilities in Soma are all hotel-based.

Makadi Bay
isolated inspiration

On a wide, sandy bay, Makadi Bay has a quiet desert setting that is perfect for those seeking to relax. Still relatively small, Makadi Bay is located 33 km (20 miles) south of Hurghada. A slew of new resorts is planned for this section of Red Sea coast. The aim is to achieve the same levels of success and development as El Gouna.

THINGS TO SEE & DO
Like all other Red Sea resorts, Makadi Bay offers watersports, diving, shopping and dining options, albeit on a much smaller scale than other towns. The scuba diving and snorkelling are excellent, but if activity is what you want, you are better off going to the more established locations of El Gouna, Hurghada and Sharm el-Sheikh. Almost all activities in Makadi Bay are resort- and hotel-based.

◄ *The beautiful white, sandy beach at Makadi Bay*

Port Safaga
point of pilgrimage

Once known for the restorative health properties of its sandy beaches, Port Safaga is now more recognized as the main departure point for Egyptians embarking on the annual *haj*. During this period, thousands of pilgrims arrive from points throughout the Nile Valley on their way to Mecca – and finding anywhere to stay can be like trying to find a needle in a haystack.

ORIENTATION

There are approximately 10 holiday villages and camps that call Port Safaga home – all of them situated on a slip road that curves off the main road coming in from the north. These camps cater to groups on diving holidays and day-trippers from other resorts like Hurghada and Soma Bay who are looking for a new underwater location to explore.

The town proper begins approximately 3 km (nearly 2 miles) after the turn-off to the holiday properties. It's a functional city, and an extremely busy port. As such, little has been built with aesthetics in mind.

THINGS TO SEE & DO
Diving ★
Safaga's main attraction is its reefs. Situated just north of the port, they are the town's one and only point of interest. In order to see the celebrated coral, you must book ahead. Boats and instructors at the main diving centre are usually booked by private groups, although they can sometimes take extra passengers on board if you give them a few days notice. Equipment costs extra.

Dive sites The major diving grounds are located 6–8 km (3–5 miles) offshore between Safaga village and Ras Abu Soma. The most common diving point is Tubiya Island, which is ringed with coral just off its beach. Other locations include the sunken North and South Fairway Reefs, the Seven Pillars off Ras Abu Soma, Shark Point, Tubiya Kemir, Gamul Soraya,

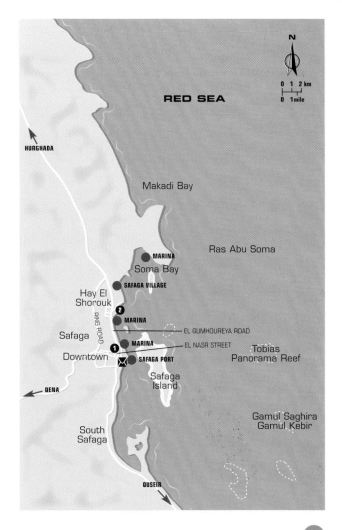

Gamul Kebir, Tubiya Soraya and Panorama Reef. All of these sites have fantastic coral, but strong currents make them suitable only for more experienced divers.

◗ *Diving on the coral reefs can be very rewarding*

Hammerhead sharks The waters around Safaga are notorious for the number of hammerhead sharks prevalent in the area. These sharks have a reputation for being aggressive. Scientists believe they track their prey by judging vibrations in the water and bouncing electromagnetic fields off their target. Check with your dive centre for latest safety information.

Windsurfing ★

Safaga is notorious for being very windy because breezes frequently gather pace when they race down the coast from the north. Windsurfing centres in the resort take advantage of this opportune fact by offering rentals by the hour or day. The best-known place, with the most well-maintained equipment, is the Shama Safaga Village, north of town. Kitesurfing is also available.

RESTAURANTS (see map on page 31)

As Port Safaga is an industrial town, tourists are not as well taken care of as they are in other Red Sea resort communities. Plans are afoot to create dozens of new resorts both north and south of town. Until that happens, you will have to stick to dining establishments that are in existing hotels. A couple of the better options include:

Cleopatra's E£ ❶ A small pizzeria that is attached to the hotel of the same name – and one of the only places in town with a bar. ⓐ Hurghada–Safaga Road ⓣ 065 25 39 26 ⓘ Cash only

Holiday Inn Safaga Palace E££ ❷ If you can't face another dinner of *fuul*, then the Holiday Inn's international restaurants are your best option. It's worth noting that some of the dishes may not be exactly what you thought they'd be – but the tastes will be recognizable. ⓣ 065 25 28 21 ⓘ Cards accepted

Marsa Alam
remote relaxation

Once a remote fishing village, Marsa Alam is essentially 'the end of the line' for holidaymakers looking for a Red Sea resort combining diving with decadence. Located 132 km (82 miles) south of El-Quesir, it is an area that is fast changing. With a new international airport planned, and many new hotels, it is rapidly becoming much more than a fishing village. The Egyptian government's desire to develop as much as possible along the Red Sea coast is also contributing strongly towards this development.

ANCIENT HISTORY
For thousands of years there has been a road from Marsa Alam to the temple village of Edfu 230 km (143 miles) across the desert to the west. The current paved road follows the line of an ancient trail that linked the Nile Valley with the Red Sea that was originally built by Ptolemy II. Emeralds and gold were mined in the region, making it a rich revenue source for the Pharaohs. Criminals and political prisoners were worked literally to death under the searing rays of the sun. Precious jewels have since been replaced by phosphate, though the mining way of life remains hard.

THE ROAD TO SOMEWHERE
The paving of the road between Edfu and Marsa Alam was completed fairly recently. Tourists must still travel in a guarded convoy between the two points due to the threat of bandits. The trip, however, is awe-inspiring. Aside from the occasional camel, the landscape is raw and deserted – just as it should be. While your hotel is sure to be filled with all modern conveniences, there are still a few things that technology hasn't touched. Mobile phones do not work in this corner of the world, so your moment of embracing sea and sand won't be disturbed by annoying ring tones.

◀ *The unspoilt reef-lined coast of Marsa Alam*

THINGS TO SEE & DO
Diving ★

If you're a serious diver, don't come to Marsa Alam. The diving community is only just starting out in this tiny hotspot and the reefs further to the north are much more interesting. For other divers the best dive centre worth organizing a trip with is the **Red Sea Diving Safari**, a tour operator committed to the protection of the local environment.
☎ 012 33 71 833

It is possible to stay on site, although accommodation tends to be extremely basic – we're talking tents and stone huts. A night here is a great antidote to the glitz and luxury one tends to associate with this part of the world.

Another centre that comes recommended is the **Awlad Baraka Diving Camp** (☎ 012 32 58 869), run in conjunction with the **Deep South Diving Centre**, which is located 14 km(nearly 9 miles) south of town. This centre offers trips to the best and most remote dive sites in the south, including Elphinstone, Fury Shoal, Dolphin House and Sbu Dahab. The price of open-water diving courses can be negotiated for less if you have a large group (six or more) and are travelling in low season.

Desert safaris ★★

For trips into the desert, **Red Sea Desert Adventures** is a safari company run by a Dutch geologist and her German partner. The two have lived in Marsa Alam for over a decade and are authorities on the art and culture of local Ababda tribespeople. Tours are tailor-made and can include walking, camel rides or jeep explorations throughout the area.
☎ 012 39 93 860.

The tomb of Sayyed al-Shazli ★

Approximately 145 km (90 miles) southwest of Marsa Alam is the tomb of a 13th-century Sheikh by the name of Sayyed al-Shazli. Regarded by many as an important Sufi leader, Al-Shazli was buried in the remote desert location that he now permanently calls home due to his desire to die in a place where no-one had ever sinned. According to legend, the Prophet

Mohammed listened to the Sheikh and personally selected a location high in the mountains at Wadi Humaysara in order to answer his prayers.

In 1947, King Farouk restored the tomb and made it easier to reach by constructing an asphalt road. During periods of heightened security, however, checkpoints may sometimes turn you back.

The *moulid* ★ ★

Ten days before the Muslim feast of Eid al-Adha, a *moulid* (a festival celebrating the birthday of a saint or holy person) is held at the tomb, which eventually reaches its climax the day before Eid. Over 60,000 Sufis from across the country gather to perform *zikrs* (Koranic verses) and hundreds of tents and market stalls are pitched. In a way, it's almost like a religious Woodstock or Glastonbury.

Getting to the tomb through all the traffic can be difficult, but once you're on your way, you'll be supported by the many joyous pilgrims who are on the same route. You'll recognize them by their trucks covered in banners, and brightly coloured decorations.

Whirling dervishes ★

If you plan on attending the *moulid* in the hopes of seeing the famous Sufi whirling dervishes, you may be out of luck. Whirling dervishes follow a branch of Sufism which was founded in Turkey. This branch has never really taken off in Egypt and in fact is sometimes thought of as blasphemous by orthodox Muslims. Other Sufi orders boast much wider support. Stick to the tourist-focused shows in Cairo if you want to see the twirling in action.

FOOD, DRINK & NIGHTLIFE

At present, the range of dining and drinking establishments in Marsa Alam is extremely limited. As more resorts are completed, this is expected to change. Until that time, you are restricted to the facilities of the various hotels. Each resort has an 'international' restaurant serving local and European cuisine. You will also find a small disco at each property restricted for the use of hotel guests.

Berenice
the final frontier

Named after the wife of Ptolemy II on whose suggestion a trading port was established here in 275 BC, Berenice is essentially the last gasp of civilization before you reach the no-man's land of the Sudan. Regulations change almost hourly as to whether or not tourists are permitted this far south, but it is plainly obvious that the Egyptian government is keen to open up this area's stretch of coast as soon as peace and safety can be ensured.

THINGS TO SEE & DO

In 1818, the entire town was excavated and the remains of the original settlement, which was abandoned in the 5th century AD, were discovered. The most important find was a Temple of Semiramis. Most of the ruins that were uncovered are off-limits to tourists.

A museum dedicated to the preservation of Bedouin culture is also of minor interest; however, the displays are poorly maintained.

Rock climbing ★

Egypt's most challenging peaks are located just outside Berenice. Among the more difficult faces are Jebel Farayid and the Berenice Bodkin, which is the largest rock needle in North Africa and the Middle East. If you are considering a climb, it might be worth a detour to see the abandoned Emerald Mines of Wadi Sakait, which date from Paranoiac times, if only to see the nearby Ptolemaic rock temple dedicated to Isis and Serapis.

Shalateen ★

This tiny town 90 km (55 miles) south of Berenice marks the administrative boundary between Egypt and the Sudan. As such, permission to visit can be hard to obtain. The town holds a weekly camel market that is worth a look. Some of the best dive sites in the Red Sea are located just offshore. Dive centres further north (particularly those based in Safaga and Marsa Alam) make arrangements to visit when possible.

Dahab
Goa by the Red Sea

**Jagged mountains meet a turquoise sea at a series of tawny beaches
known as Dahab, located 95 km (59 miles) north of Sharm el-Sheikh. The
name 'Dahab' is derived from the Arabic word for gold, an apt name
drawn from the glow of the golden sands that stretch as far as the eye
can see. It's an intriguing resort town, divided almost evenly between
holiday villages designed for high-end visitors and a Bedouin settlement
that attracts younger, more adventurous travellers. A third region is
developing to the north, though resorts are still awaiting completion.**

DAHAB CITY
As the main commercial centre of the region, Dahab City is far from
inspiring. Tourists will find little apart from the post office and bank,
a supermarket and a branch of the tourist police (opposite the Novotel).

Most tourists arriving in Dahab head straight to the more salubrious
trappings of Asilah. Taxis swarm around the bus station at every hour of
the day hoping to pick up passengers for the journey. A taxi ride should
be inexpensive – less if you share with others.

ASILAH
Dahab's reputation as a bit of a hippie haven is due more to the happenings
at Asilah than the city that gives the region its name. Asilah's history
of laid-back lushness dates back to the 1960s when Israeli troops began
arriving for a spot of rest and relaxation. The local Bedouins didn't know
what hit them. Today, the Bedouin village that once existed is gone,
replaced by concrete buildings, restaurants and campgrounds.

If you are hoping to visit Egypt as an independent traveller, Asilah
is the right place, as it caters to solo visitors largely due to the fact that
it lacks the massive resorts and package tourists found in other locales.
Sadly, the area has also grown up since the days when it was a sleepy dot
on the Red Sea coast. Where once there were isolated beaches, a paved
'Corniche' offering camel rides and beach umbrellas now lies.

Buckets of charm

Asilah continues to draw visitors hoping to take a step back from life – and they often remain longer than they ever intended. While it lacks the incredible diving of Sharm or the facilities of Hurghada, it makes up for it with buckets of charm.

You may be seduced into thinking that Asilah is a haven of hedonism. If this thought is drawing you, then you may want to think again. Asilah is still in Egypt and there are rules you must follow. Women who sunbathe can do so without hassle, but if you attempt to go topless, you will be arrested. There are also regular crackdowns on dope smoking and if you are caught, you may face serious trouble (see page 42).

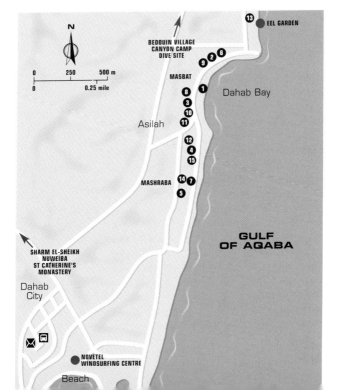

HEALTH & HAPPINESS

The local Bedouin have a long history of smuggling hashish into Egypt through Dahab. When foreign hippies discovered the tradition back in the 1970s, they flocked to the area, drawn to the abundance of drug supplies. Business flourished in the 1980s following the handover of the Sinai to Egypt because the local police force became involved, accepting numerous kickbacks to keep production protected. If you decide to partake, you are on your own when it comes to the police. Carrying even a minimal amount of hashish will result in jail, fines or worse. Whatever anyone may tell you, smoking dope is not legal. Avoid scam-artists at all costs, particularly Europeans and Israelis who may try to convince you that they can be trusted because they aren't 'local'.

THINGS TO SEE & DO

Diving ★

While dive sites aren't as filled with fish as those off Sharm or Hurghada, there are several locations well worth exploring. There are over 40 dive clubs in town offering a wide range of possibilities. Shore diving is the norm, with reefs reached by pick-ups. The best are north of Dahab Bay, just past the lagoon. Asilah offers fewer options, except for the area around the light-house. Most divers in the know head 7–8 km (around 5 miles) up the coast to Eel Garden, Canyon and Blue Hole.

Daily trips to these sites can be arranged through almost every dive centre. Two of the better ones are the Fantasea Dive Centre (☎ 069 64 00 43) and Fish & Friends (☎ 069 64 06 72). Be sure to choose your club carefully as some of the centres have lousy reputations and poor safety standards. Ask around if you are unsure.

Diving excursions

Blue Hole For experienced divers, the Blue Hole is the challenge of a life-time. Every year, this incredible site claims several lives. It's a spectacular shaft that plunges down 80 m (260 ft). The challenge involves descending 60 m (197 ft) and swimming through a transverse passage to come up on the other side. Divers who ascend too quickly risk 'the bends'. If you worry about your skill level, stay close to the surface and work your way around to a dip in the reef known as the Bridge. There's plenty to see – you can even view the schools of fish and corals with snorkelling gear.

🛈 Warning – inexperienced divers should not attempt this dive.

Canyon The Canyon is a dark, narrow fissure reached by swimming along the reef from the shore and then diving to the edge of a coral wall. Inexperienced divers should not attempt this dive as it sinks to a depth of 50 m (190 ft). If you do want to attempt the site, there is still plenty to see at the top of the reef – just be sure to know your limits before you go.

Mashraba As one of the easiest reefs to reach from the coast, the reef at the northern end of Mashraba is a popular diving spot. Unfortunately, its popularity has resulted in a lot of rubbish in the surrounding waters. If you can ignore the litter, you'll find a series of nice table corals teeming with fish life. There are also reefs off the southern end of Mashraba, just before the lagoon, however, they are not considered as desirable.

Ras Abu Gallum This protected area, a 30 km (18 mile) stretch of coastline with three diving beaches accessed by jeep or camel, is the main day-long dive destination, with deep virgin reefs with a variety of corals and fish. Snorkellers can sometimes be accommodated by the dive centre.

Nabq Shahin Nabq Shahin is definitely the site of choice for the pros. Turbulent seas make this spot off-limits to all but the most experienced – the slightest breeze can make it an absolute no-go area. A difficult journey does have a fantastic payoff: fantastic coral and fish of every colour of the rainbow.

Lobster fishing ★ ★ ★

You'll have to be an insomniac to enjoy it, but lobster hunting is one of the more intriguing activities to try. Excursions only go at night when lobster activity is at its peak with the trip culminating in a lobster feast on the beach. Book your trip through **Hamid 'The Lobster Man'** ⓐ Crazy Camel Camp ⓣ 069 64 06 62

Camel or jeep safaris ★

For a short trip along the beach, you can rent out camels, or horses if you are happy to pay more. Longer trips are just as easy to arrange, thanks to a plethora of guides. Try to find a Bedouin guide as they know more than a trans-planted Egyptian. Guiding is also a major

◐ Jeep safari

source of revenue for the Bedouin community. Look for camel drivers along the waterfront, but be sure to register your trip with the local police before you set off, and don't pay the camel driver until you return to town.

The **Centre for Sinai** (ⓣ 069 64 07 02) offers trips into the interior and tries to promote local culture. Even if you don't want a formal tour, it's still a great source for private guides. **Man and the Environment Dahab** is another outfit worth checking out. ⓣ 069 64 10 91

Specific locations that are offered on itineraries to the interior are the **Coloured Canyon** and **Nabq Mangrove Forest** (see pages 52 and 79).

Windsurfing ★ ★

Dahab has great winds for windsurfing, which blow for up to 200 days per year. The windsurfing centre at the **Novotel** offers courses as well as daily rentals.

Meet the locals ★★★

Fifty thousand Bedouin call the Sinai peninsula home. It's a harsh and unforgiving environment to live in, especially in the north where most choose to congregate. There are 14 distinct tribes, all with ties across the Middle East to families in the Negev, Jordan and Saudi Arabia.

Tribal rhythms The largest Bedouin tribe in the Sinai are the Sukwarka. The centre of their community is Al-Arish on the Mediterranean coast, so while they make up a large proportion of the Bedouin population, you will probably have the least contact with them if you are sticking to the Red Sea resort communities. Other important tribes scattered throughout the north and centre of the peninsula are the Tarabin, the Tyaha and the Haweitat.

Southern friends The seven tribes in the south are collectively known as the Towara or 'Arabs of Al-Tor'. Members of these tribes work as guides for tourists wishing to travel into the Sinai interior. However, many of the major tour operators refuse to work with them out of mistrust.

Guiding the way Hiring a Bedouin tour guide is actually quite easy. There are locations in most Red Sea resort communities where they gather collectively waiting for trade. Choosing a Bedouin guide not only ensures that you will be getting the best possible guide for your safari, but you will also be helping the Bedouin community who rely on the income.

Bridging the cultural gap An invitation from a Bedouin guide or family should be treasured. Bedouins have fascinating traditions and a highly developed understanding of the environment. While the food at a banquet may not be to your particular taste – shall we say 'sheep eyes, anyone?' – you will treasure the memories of your experience. And you'll have made lifelong friends at the same time.

RESTAURANTS (see map on page 41)

Al Capone £££ ❶ Why this restaurant is named after a Chicago gangster is a mystery. Perhaps it's due to the fact that if the mobster could choose anywhere to escape, it might be to this relaxing fish restaurant where all the things on the menu are sold by weight. The staff encourage patrons to spend as long as they like in the restaurant – they don't mind even if you get up from your table in the middle of the meal to have a swim in the Gulf of Aqaba. ➌ Asilah waterfront ❶ Cash only

Carm Inn £££ ❷ A great establishment serving Indonesian food, in addition to Indian and Western options. Ingredients are fresh, which is reflected in the incredible flavours. ➌ Masbat ❶ 069 64 13 00 ❶ Cards accepted

Crazy House £££ ❸ For the best fish in town, there's no other place to go except Crazy House. The fish are displayed out front and sold by weight. Service is rather slow, so it's best not to go if you're famished. Crazy House's waterfront location encourages people to spend hours passing the day. The fact that it's one of the only places by the sea with tables and chairs doesn't hurt either. ➌ Asilah waterfront ❶ Cash only

Dolphin Camp Café £££ ❹ Indian cuisine and Balti dishes served to relaxed diners on the waterfront. Vegetarians are well catered for. Low cushions invite diners to spend hours lounging comfortably between courses. ➌ Mashraba ❶ 069 64 00 18 ❶ Cash only

Jasmine Pension £££ ❺ This busy establishment dishes up food like an Egyptian momma used to make. Located directly on the water, it's a great place to spend an evening watching the sunset. Meals are large and filling. ➌ Mashraba ❶ 069 64 03 70 ❶ Cash only

◀ *Enjoy lunch on the beach*

Jays Restaurant E£ ❻ Incredibly cheap British-run establishment that dishes up Egyptian and Western fare. The menu changes every week according to what is fresh and available. No alcohol is served but the variety of items makes a change of pace from that on offer everywhere else in town. ⓐ Masbat ☎ 012 33 53 377 ⓘ Cash only

Lakhabita E££ ❼ This Egyptian restaurant appeals to the hippie and eccentric in all of us. The décor is decidedly exotic, with Egyptian furniture packing the place to the rafters. The food matches the décor with numerous traditional dishes on the menu. There are also some Asian and European-inspired meals that are best left avoided. ⓐ Mashraba ☎ 010 19 64 120 ⓘ Cards accepted

Neptune Restaurant E££ ❽ Neptune is Dahab's only Chinese restaurant. If you're looking for authenticity, go elsewhere. Westernized 'sweet and sour' dishes and basic noodles are what's on offer. ⓐ Masbat ☎ 069 64 02 62 ⓘ Cash only

Shark's Restaurant E£ ❾ A great spot for vegetarians that is suitable for all budgets. ⓐ Masbat ☎ 010 56 10 023 ⓒ Dinner only. No alcohol. ⓘ Cash only.

Tota Restaurant E££ ❿ This popular restaurant is shaped like a boat and serves up delicious Italian food. Pizzas are large, if a bit light on toppings; the lasagne is particularly recommended. Try for a table on the top 'deck' to enjoy the sunset while sipping a drink. Happy hour (17.00–19.00) is the time to go when bottles of Stella cost just E£6. ⓐ Masbat ☎ 069 64 00 14 ⓘ Cards accepted

Trattoria Pizzeria E£ ⓫ It's a mystery why pizza is so popular in Egyptian resort towns, but if they all tasted like those served at Trattoria Pizzeria, you would wonder no longer. This two-storey pizzeria does pizza better than anyone else in a variety of crusts. Other Italian dishes are also available. ⓐ Masbat ☎ 069 64 01 73 ⓘ Cash only

NIGHTLIFE

Unlike other Red Sea resorts, Dahab isn't known for its nightlife. Things stay pretty quiet after dark in these parts – and for this reason many travellers want to go there. Not for the hippies the flashing lights, loud music and drunken revelry of Sharm and Hurghada. A party with trance music under the stars is more their idea of a good time. If you're looking for a drink and a disco, the following are your best bets:

Al-Zar Bar **12** If you need a place to relax, the trance-like atmosphere and scented candles of this hippy hangout will certainly seduce you. If not, the beachside location and lull of the waves certainly will. ⓐ Mashraba ❶ 069 64 00 18 ❶ Cash only

Crazy House **9** The billiard table and waterside location in the heart of Asilah pull in the punters. Beer is cheap and draws a diverse crowd, and serves fish and chips (see page 47). ⓐ Asilah waterfront ❶ Cash only

Furry Cup **13** This is the hotspot where Dahab's diving instructors come to mix and mingle. It's also a great place to pick up advice on which dive centres are better than others. A lively atmosphere is guaranteed almost every day of the week and the music is always good. ⓐ Blue Beach Club, Asilah ❶ 069 64 04 13 ❶ Cards accepted

New Sphinx Bar **14** Get away from the Masbat scene with a drink at the New Sphinx. It's a well-stocked bar with happy hour (17.00–19.00). ⓐ New Sphinx Hotel, Shat El Mashrabey ❶ 069 64 04 94

Shipwreck Bar **15** A great rooftop bar with wonderful views of the water. Happy hour is 19.00–20.00 and the place gets packed. ⓐ Nesima Resort, Mashraba ❶ 069 64 03 20 ❶ Cash only

Tota Restaurant **10** This boat-shaped Italian restaurant transforms into a disco as the evening hours progress. Explore the upper deck if you're looking for a boogie. ⓐ Masbat ❶ 069 64 00 14 ❶ Cards accepted

Nuweiba
cheap chic

The resort of Nuweiba benefits from a spectacular setting right on the coast of the Gulf of Aqaba. With its rugged mountains and sandy beaches, it is well worth visiting, especially as it is probably one of the cheapest places for a holiday anywhere in the country.

Before the Palestinian *intifada* of September 2000, Israelis constituted the bulk of visitors to this prime stretch of real estate. After this time, Israelis abandoned the area and the tourism industry all but died. The Iraq war hasn't helped either, resulting in low occupancy rates and a guaranteed warm welcome wherever you go in town.

Resorts are strung out over a long distance thanks to a lack of town planning. There is no real centre to Nuweiba and many developments have been left half complete following the collapse of local businesses. The resorts that are left are of a high quality and incredibly affordable. It's a great place to mix and mingle with travellers moving onwards to the Israeli border and affluent Egyptians, who consider the town to be an affordable and more authentic resort community which is preferable to Nama Bay.

ORIENTATION
Nuweiba is divided into three sections. To the south is the bus station, port, banks and the massive Hilton Coral Resort. **Nuweiba City**, 8 km (5 miles) north is a spread-out settlement of tourist shops, bazaars, hotels and cheap eateries. As more hotels are being constructed, the gap between Nuweiba City and the port is diminishing.

Further north is **Tarabin**. This neighbourhood, named after the local Bedouin tribe for which it is home. It is dominated by its stretch of beach, which is is filled with small hotels and lined with bamboo-and-concrete huts. Less tranquil then it used to be, it caters predominantly to a travelling crowd looking to shun the big resorts of the area or stopping off en route to the Israeli border.

THINGS TO SEE & DO
Camel and jeep treks ★ ★ ★

After St Catherine's (see page 82), Nuweiba is probably the best location from which to organize a trip to see the Sinai peninsula. Local Bedouin guides offer a wide range of camel or jeep safaris from town with itineraries that feature a number of key destinations.

Durations depend on your chosen itinerary and mode of transport. Camels may feel more authentic, but they will also take two to three times longer than a jeep, and it takes some getting used to their swaying gait.

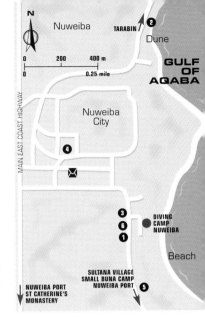

Guides and destinations Prices for guides per day can vary quite considerably, with camel journeys priced at the high end of the scale. This price should include meals and the cost of registering the trip with the police. Drinking water may or may not be included. Make sure you check before you go as the further you travel away from 'civilization', the more expensive it will be to replenish.

Choose your guide or tour operator carefully. You can literally book a package from any camp and supermarket in Tarabin. Your best bet will probably be with a local Bedouin guide. Not only are they marginalized by local tour operators, they also know the region far better than anyone else.

There are literally dozens of places a safari can go, but some of the more popular destinations are listed below. For detailed descriptions of some of the more major sites, see the Excursions section of the book, starting on page 71.

Coloured Canyon ★ ★

The Coloured Canyon lies between St Catherine and Nuweiba, and derives its name from the layers of bright, multicoloured stones that resemble paintings on its steep, narrow walls. It is quite sheltered from the wind, which makes it eerily silent – except when the large tour groups descend. It's a popular day-trip from Sinai's resorts, so it is worth making an effort to arrive early in the day or late in the afternoon when the masses aren't there. Changes to this policy of 'come one, come all' are in motion. As the canyon falls under the boundaries of the Taba Protectorate, there are discussions underway to control crowds through payment of an entrance fee and implementation of daily number limits.

Ain al-Furtega ★

A pleasing palm oasis located only 16 km (10 miles) from Nuweiba and easily accessible in a day. Its proximity to Nuweiba means it is usually the first port of call for any trekkers.

Ain Khudra ★ ★

A famously beautiful spring fringed with date palms. Legend has it that it is the location of the biblical Hazeroth, where Miriam was stricken with leprosy for criticizing Moses. It's an easy day trip by jeep.

Ain Umm Ahmed ★ ★

The largest oasis in the Eastern Sinai. Ain Umm Ahmed is known for its abundant palm trees, Bedouin community, and stream. The stream becomes an icy torrent in the winter months when it is fed by the snow on the highest peaks on the Sinai.

Gebel Barga ★ ★

If you are a climber, then Gebel Barga should be a must. The climb is difficult (and therefore recommended only for those with at least some experience), but the stunning views over the eastern Sinai make the trek worthwhile. This trip is further away from other destinations. Budgeting two to three days for the return journey is recommended.

Mayat el-Wishwashi ★

Once the largest rainwater cistern in the Sinai, Mayat has been reduced to a trickle. Go after the annual floods, when the water level rises and there is much more to look at.

Mayat Malkha ★

Surrounded by colourful sandstone, Mayat Malkha is a palm grove fed by the waters of Mayat el-Wishwashi, which is much more lush during the flood season.

Wadi Huweiyit ★★

A colourful canyon that offers panoramic views over to Saudi Arabia.

Wadi Sheikh Atiya ★

This peaceful spot is the final resting place of the father of the Tarabin tribe, the largest Bedouin tribe in this region. There is a small oasis here and it is a popular destination for Bedouin pilgrimages.

Bedouin wedding ★★★

All-night Bedouin weddings are worth attending if you manage to find a guide who knows one that you can be invited to. These colourful functions provide a rare opportunity for young Bedouin men and women to mix and mingle. The guide Anis Anisan at **El Khan Camp** is reliable and well-known for organizing invitations to such events. ☏ 069 50 03 19

Horse riding ★★

It's possible to rent horses by the hour at the upmarket beach resort of Bawaki, located approximately 20 km (12 miles) up the coast from Tarabin. Rentals are reaonably cheap.

Diving and water sports ★

Nuweiba is not as focused on diving as the other Sinai resorts. There are still underwater areas worth exploring, many of them tailor-made for beginners. Shallow reefs offshore, such as the Stone House beyond the

● *There are plenty of places to hire snorkelling gear*

southern promontory are perfect for snorkellers. Divers tend to head out to Ras Abu Gallum on day trips. Dives can be arranged through any of the four dive centres in Nuweiba.

Camping ★★

Nuweiba is popular for camping. There are dozens of secure camp-grounds where you can pitch a tent, enjoy Bedouin meals and sit under the stars, lulled by the sound of the waves. If you don't have a tent, there are huts that you can rent out. Habiba Camp and Small Duna close to Nuweiba City are recommended. Check in advance that it isn't a day when they are expecting tour groups from Sharm if you want peace and relaxation.

RESTAURANTS (see map on page 51)

Bedouin Restaurant E££ ❶ Dig in to delicious fish and Egyptian-style mezze at this eatery with a strong Bedouin theme. Try and avoid it on a night when large tour groups fill the place – which is more often than you might like. ⓐ Nuweiba City ⓣ 069 50 00 82 ⓘ Cash only

Blue Bus E££ ❷ The Blue Bus is widely thought of as the best place to eat in Tarabin. It's one of the longest established dining spots on the Tarabin strip, serving reasonable pizzas, pastas and fish. Beachside location. ⓐ Tarabin strip ⓣ 069 50 01 72 ⓘ Cash only

Cleopatra Restaurant E££ ❸ Good fish dishes and Egyptian mezze are served at this establishment located opposite the Domina Nuweiba Hotel. Basic, but filling. ⓐ Nuweiba City ⓣ 069 50 05 03 ⓘ Cash only

Dr Shishkebab E£ ❹ This dining establishment serves probably the largest portions in town. Each item on the menu comes with side orders of mouth-watering *ta'amiyya*, *hummus*, salad and aubergines. You may hit an evening when the owner puts on an impromptu concert with his friends. ⓐ Bazaar, Nuweiba City ⓣ 069 50 02 73 ⓘ Cash only

Habiba Camp E££ ❺ This restaurant at the campsite of the same name serves tasty buffet lunches that cater to the day-trip brigade. ⓐ Nuweiba City ⓣ 069 50 07 70 ⓘ Cash only

Han Kang E£££ ❻ Surprisingly good Chinese–Korean eatery opposite the Helnan. Basic 'Oriental' cuisine to more intricate dishes are available. ⓐ Nuweiba City ⓣ 069 50 09 70 ⓘ Cash only

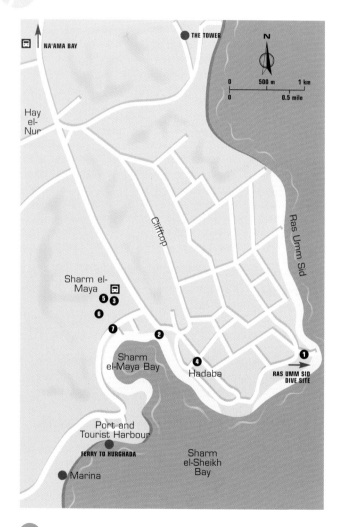

Sharm el-Sheikh
dive right in

The resort town of Sharm el-Sheikh didn't really exist until it was created by the Israelis in 1967 after they captured the Sinai in the 1967 war. Built to break the Egyptian blockade of the Tiran strait, the town developed slowly until divers 'discovered' the wealth of reefs located just offshore in the late 1970s.

Today, Sharm is one of Egypt's biggest tourist hotspots. The resort is actually a collection of areas, including the high-end luxury locale of Na'ama Bay and the more workaday downtown core of Sharm el-Maya. Diving remains one of the biggest draws of the area and there are plenty of operators who offer packages for both beginners and those who have more advanced skills. Though there are beaches, holidaymakers are advised to stick to private hotel beaches in order to avoid attracting unwanted attention.

ORIENTATION
The name Sharm el-Sheikh refers to a town that actually does not exist. Rather, it's a collection of neighbourhoods, each one of which has a very different flavour.

Sharm el-Maya
Sharm el-Maya is Sharm el-Sheikh's commercial core and home to the large market area, port and marina. If you're on a budget, then this is the part of town to explore if you're looking for a place to rest your head. As the neighbourhood is traditionally Egyptian in feel, it is advised that you dress modestly when exploring the area.

Na'ama Bay
The major resort community of Na'ama Bay is located 7 km (4.3 miles) up the coast. Most of the five-star resorts and nightlife are located here. The sandy beaches are wide and well-tended in Na'ama and the feeling is

much more like a Mediterranean resort. You should feel comfortable wearing beachwear in all corners of this glamour spot, however, you should still avoid wearing bathing costumes away from the beach or pool.

Ras Umm Sid

South-east of Sharm el-Maya is the location of the next phase of development for the region. A string of hotels and resorts are being constructed along the roadside, in various stages of readiness. The area stretches from the Ras Umm Sid dive site north to a dive site known as The Tower. Resorts in this region vary in quality, with the high-end properties closer to the beach.

Residential neighbourhoods

Adjacent to downtown Sharm el-Maya is an upper-class residential neighbourhood on a cliffside called Hadaba. There is little here to attract the attention of tourists. Another residential neighbourhood, known as Hay el-Nur, lies further north and is designed for the middle classes. Here is where you will find the bus station, hospital and a well-stocked supermarket.

THINGS TO SEE & DO

Shark Bay ★★

Located 10 km (6 miles) up the coast from Na'ama is Shark Bay. Once a secluded getaway from the hustle and bustle of Sharm, the location is now packed with large holiday villages. A sandy track was once the only way you could reach the area. Today, the track has been replaced by a series of tarmacked roads, mostly used to service the hotels and shuttle holidaymakers back and forth to Na'ama or the airport.

Despite the name, Shark Bay has no sharks to speak of – they were all scared off by divers long ago. Left behind are a lovely selection of tropical fish attracted by the coral gardens just offshore. If you are visiting from other resorts, you will have to pay a charge to use the beach. This fee includes the use of the showers and one soft drink.

SHOPPING

Shopping in Sharm is restricted to a number of modern malls and faux 'souqs' designed to look like markets of yesteryear. If the thermometer is rising, the shopping malls are a good place to revive as almost all of them are air-conditioned.

Little in Sharm can't be found somewhere else in the country, and what you can find will invariably cost double what you would spend in Cairo or Luxor.

Some of the more interesting shops to check out include **Aladdin** at the Camel Hotel for arts and crafts, **Bashayer** in the Sharm Mall for products from Upper Egypt and **Karkade** (also in Sharm Mall) for spices, oils, herbs and 'antiques'.

◆ *Testing the water in Shark Bay*

Sinai Wildlife Clinic ★ ★

Visit this non-profit organization to see how locals are attempting to conserve the native wildlife. In autumn, the most important work is done and volunteers are taken on to help work on the clinic's various projects. Those with veterinary or nursing skills are especially welcome. Ring in advance for details ☎ 069 60 16 10 ext 241

Diving ★

Dive centres are two a penny in Sharm, especially in Na'ama Bay. An extensive range of courses, trips, and equipment is all available. Due to the stiff competition, all of the centres are generally recommended. Prices and operating styles do vary so it is worth shopping around for the best deals.

Costs and packages Those new to diving should try an introductory dive before they commit to full lessons. Expect to pay £25–35 (US$45–60) including equipment.

If you get the bug, a five-day, open-water diving course is the next step. Any good course must include classroom theory. This will then lead to dives in a hotel swimming pool or just offshore followed by a couple of boat-dives at the end. One of the most affordable and respected open-water PADI courses is offered by **Anemone** at the **Pigeon House Hotel** ☎ 069 60 09 99

More advanced divers are also spoiled for choice. Almost all of the dive clubs and centres have courses that will train you to become an instructor, or offer specialised skills such as underwater navigation and night diving. Prices may vary significantly depending on the type of course, demand and time of year.

Liveaboards If you are already PADI-certified and want to do a lot of boat diving, dive packages or liveaboards are recommended. A five-day dive package, including two dives per day will cost from around £130 (US$230).

Liveaboards offer more options and will take avid divers to places other boats just can't reach. Average costs are approximately £55 (US$100) per person, per day for a boat of four to six air-conditioned cabins, including full board, airport transfers, tanks and weights. Diving equipment and alcohol will be extra.

Diving operators For a full list of qualified diving operators in the Sharm area, contact the **Sharm Diving Union** on ℹ️ 069 66 04 18.

Diving excursions

Sharm is world-renowned for its diving. There is an amazing selection of dive spots in the region, which act as the major attraction for holiday-makers to this popular resort.

Amphoras This diving point gets its name from a cargo of clay jars found on an Ottoman ship that sunk on this reef. Luckily, the jars remain sealed as they contain mercury. This is an easy dive and can be negotiated by those new to undersea diving.

Paradise Paradise is a 20-minute sail north of Sharm. This dive site is visually spectacular and filled with vibrant colour. Many believe that it must have been an underwater photographer who gave this site its name due to the amazing picture opportunities. Paradise is a good place to spot sea turtles as they search for food.

Pinky's Wall Exactly halfway between Sharm and Na'ama Bay, Pinky's Wall is a wall that plunges into the blue depths of the sea. The reef is broken by vertical cracks and crevices. This is a classic wall dive as the coral wall drops away as far as the eye can see right from the surface.

Ras Umm Sid The easiest site to reach is Ras Umm Sid. This location is composed almost entirely of coral reef. However, Sharm's booming resort construction has caused some pollution to this stretch of waterfront.

○ *Coral reefs are a main attraction of Sharm el-Sheikh*

The Tower A pleasant diving beach headlined by the Tower hotel. A coral pillar located just offshore drops 60 m (196 ft) into the sea depths and draws a mass of experienced divers.

Turtle Bay Less of a diving spot than a gentle location for a snorkel and swim. The bay gets its name from green turtles that used to populate the area. Sadly, few of the creatures can be spotted today.

Reef protection

The development of large resorts on the Red Sea coastline may be bene-
ficial to tourists in terms of offering them more selection, but they also
have an impact on the environment. The coral reefs that originally
attracted travellers to the region are threatened – but there are plenty
of things you can do to ensure that the glorious reefs can be visited by
generations to come.

Keep it clean Almost the entire Egyptian coastline is now a government
protectorate, as is the Red Sea coast from Hurghada south to Sudan.
What this means is that you can be penalised if you violate any of the
code of ethics determined by the government as necessary to keep the
reef safe from harm. These code laws include:

- Do not collect, remove or damage any material, living or dead (includ-
  ing coral, fish and plants).
- Do not stir up sand as it is difficult for coral to remove sand particles
  and may result in stunted growth over a long period.
- Do not litter – especially cigarette butts.
- Do not fish or spearfish. If you see others doing it, report them to the
  Egyptian National Parks Office.
- Do not walk or anchor on any reef area. Try to time snorkelling with
  the high tide so you can swim – and not walk – over the living reef.
- Do not feed the fish as this disturbs the reef's ecological balance.
- Do not touch, kneel on or kick coral as this will cause permanent,
  irreversible damage.

Cause and effect Killing the coral will eventually kill off the fish.
If you attempt to skirt the laws by breaking off coral to bring home
as a souvenir, you may be prosecuted. Please do not attempt to pay
baksheesh (a tip) to the dive centre as it is illegal. Do not be tempted
to flout these rules just because you know you can get around them.
It doesn't help anyone involved. The main rule to follow above all others
is: leave the reef how you found it.

Unwritten rules While they aren't official, there are other tips you can follow to make your diving experience have less of an impact on the environment:

- Practise maintaining proper buoyancy control. This fact is touched on very little during beginner's open-water courses, yet most of the major damage done to reefs occurs when divers descend too fast and collide with the reef. Please remember that because the Red Sea is extremely saline, you will need extra weight to overcome the heightened buoyancy.
- Take care in underwater caves. There are plenty to explore in the Red Sea, however, long periods of time spent inside them may result in your air bubbles rising up and forming pockets of gas within the roof.
- Be conscious of your fins. Avoid contact with reefs and try not to kick up too much sand.
- Do not wear gloves. Gloves are banned in Ras Mohamed National Park, but many dive centres are lax in enforcing the rule.

> **GET ADVICE**
> When in doubt as to who to dive with, one of the best sources of information is other divers. If you haven't booked your dive prior to arriving in resort, ask around at any of the local drinking dens. Chances are you will run into a few opinionated souls. True divers will speak their mind as to which centres follow the best environmental policies as they are just as eager as you are to see the reefs thrive.

RESTAURANTS (NA'AMA BAY, see map on page 65)

Andrea's E£ ❶ Cheap chicken dishes and quality Egyptian yummies. Good value makes this a great place for those on a budget. ❸ Off the main strip, next to the Hard Rock Café ❶ Cash only

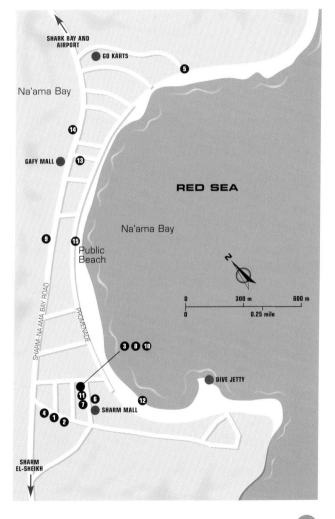

SHARK BAY AND
AIRPORT

GO KARTS

❺

Na'ama Bay

❶❹

GAFY MALL ❶❸

❾ ❶❺
Public
Beach

RED SEA

Na'ama Bay

N

0   300 m   600 m
0   0.25 mile

SHARM-NA'AMA BAY ROAD

PROMENADE

❸ ❽ ❿

DIVE JETTY

❶❶ ❻
❼
❹ ❶
❷   SHARM MALL

❶❷

SHARM
EL-SHEIKH

65

Hard Rock Café E££ ❷ Sharm's most popular nightspot is a branch of the London-based chain dedicated to the world of rock music. Expect typical hamburgers at an untypical price. A good children's menu attracts tots during the day while the 20 and 30-somethings patrol at night. ⓐ Off the main strip ☏ 069 60 26 65 ❶ Cards accepted

Mashy Café du Liban E££ ❸ Lebanese mezze and meat under the stars. Carnivores will love it. Go on an empty stomach to appreciate the food. ⓐ Sanafir Hotel ☏ 069 60 01 97 ❶ Cards accepted

La Rustichella Restaurant E£££ ❹ The best Italian food in town. This is where Italians tourists go when they want a touch of comfort food. Home-style cooking is what's on the menu. Fish dishes are highly rated. ⓐ Off the main strip ☏ 010 11 60 92 ❶ Cards accepted

Sala Thai E£££ ❺ High-end Thai food that deserves the plaudits. The nibbles are delicious, while the teak interiors and outdoor terrace are a delight. Choose a table overlooking the sea for a perfect evening. ⓐ Hyatt Regency Hotel ☏ 069 60 12 34 ❶ Cards accepted

Shin Seol E££ ❻ Passable Chinese food that will satisfy any yen you might have for fried rice or sweet-and-sour sauce. A good place for a bite if out shopping. ⓐ Sharm Mall ❶ Cash only

Tandoori E££ ❼ Pleasant Indian eatery in an outdoor courtyard location. There are a wide variety of tandoori dishes to choose from, but it's the dhal that will keep you coming back for more. ⓐ Camel Hotel ☏ 069 60 07 00 ❶ Cards accepted

La Trattoria E£££ ❽ Good quality Italian food in a restaurant run by actual Italians. Stick with the basics as fussier dishes tend to disappoint. ⓐ Sanafir Hotel ☏ 069 60 01 97 ❶ Cards accepted

NIGHTLIFE (NA'AMA BAY, see map on page 65)

Black House Disco ❾ When Bus Stop begins to bore, discoers get down at the Black Horse. The club stays open until the last clubber leaves the dance floor. ⓐ Rosetta Hotel ❶ 069 60 18 88 ❶ Cash only

Bus Stop ❿ Sharm's hottest nightclub sees a wild crowd – especially on Thursday evenings. It's the centre of the action for fans of decadence and dancing till dawn. ⓐ Sanafir Hotel ❶ 069 60 01 97 ❶ Cards accepted

Camel Dive Bar ⓫ The drinking spot of choice for serious divers. If you want to trade tips on sightings, equipment and reef quality, then this is the place to go. Amongst those in the know, it's also known as Chris's Place. ⓐ Adjoins the Camel Hotel ❶ 069 60 07 00 ❶ Cash only

La Folie Bar ⓬ Looking for a quiet drink? Then this is the place to come. Tables sit almost directly over the water taking in views of the twinkling lights of Na'ama Bay. ⓐ Iberotel Lido ❶ 069 60 26 03 ❶ Cards accepted

Harry's Bar ⓭ Expensive bar that tries way too hard to look like a British pub. The selection of beer on tap is the most extensive in town. Occasional nights offering all-you-can-drink beer for a reasonable price are worth the trip. ⓐ Marriott Hotel ❶ 069 60 01 90 ❶ Cards accepted

Pigeon House Bar ⓮ The best place in town to kick off your evening due to its daily early happy hour drink specials, but it can get very packed. ⓐ Sharm–Na'ama Bay Road ❶ 069 60 09 96 ❶ Cash only

Pirates Bar ⓯ This is another bar for dedicated divers. More geared towards long-term residents and locals, the place has a cheesy nautical theme. Drinks are discounted by 30 per cent between 17:30 and 19:30. ⓐ Hilton Fayrouz Hotel ❶ 069 60 01 40 ❶ Cards accepted

Rooftop Bar ❿ Feel like a sultan as you recline on cushions under the stars. ⓐ Sanafir Hotel ❶ 069 60 01 97 ❶ Cards accepted

RESORTS

RESTAURANTS (SHARM EL-SHEIKH, see map on page 56)

Al-Fanar E£££ **❶** The place to go for a romantic meal, Al-Fanar boasts a beautiful waterfront location at the base of a lighthouse. Italian meals are served Bedouin-style under the stars. Go for the views more than the food. **ⓐ** Ras Umm Sid **ⓣ** 069 66 22 18 **ⓘ** Cash only

Al Taib E£££ **❷** Great seafood spot located in a lush garden on a hillside. All the food is uniformly fresh and tasty. **ⓐ** Sharm el-Maya **ⓣ** 010 55 76 86 **ⓘ** Cash only

Fisherman's Café E£££ **❸** If you're after something filling, this café dishes up simple chicken and fish dishes and generous side orders. Alcohol available. **ⓐ** Sharm el-Maya **ⓣ** 069 55 03 57 **ⓘ** Cash only

Kafr Amarein E£££ **❹** Egyptian seafood restaurant that is good if you need to find a table on a busy evening. The large size of the establishment can more than accommodate most groups. **ⓐ** Sharm Inn, Hadaba **ⓣ** 069 66 33 22 **ⓘ** Cash only

King E£ **❺** Quick and easy *fuul* and *ta'amiyya* takeaway in the heart of the market. Great for a fast lunch or late-evening bite. **ⓐ** Sharm el-Maya market **ⓘ** Cash only

Safsara Restaurant E£££ **❻** Probably the most well-loved restaurant in town, the Safsara is celebrated for its seafood. Family run and extremely small, this eatery only has eight tables which are full at all hours. Recommended dishes include *calamari* and *babaghanoug* (see page 95). **ⓐ** Sharm el-Maya **ⓣ** 069 66 04 74 **ⓘ** No alcohol. Cash only

Sinai Star E£££ **❼** This popular seafood restaurant is especially well-liked by tour groups. Fish dishes are particularly recommended. Beer is not available on the menu, but if you ask nicely, they will get a waiter to run to a nearby shop to pick up a few bottles for you. **ⓐ** Sharm el-Maya **ⓣ** 069 66 03 23 **ⓘ** Cash only

Taba
gateway to Egypt

Since 1982, Taba has served as the main border crossing point between Egypt and Israel. Other than a café, a small stretch of beach and a single luxury hotel, little exists at the moment to attract tourists to visit the town – but the Egyptian government is doing as much as it can to change all that.

About 17 km (10.5 miles) south of Taba, a new development of luxury hotels is being constructed in the ritzy location dubbed 'Taba Heights'. When complete, it will house a casino (geared mainly towards Israeli day-trippers), shops, bars, restaurants, a medical clinic and water park. The Egyptian government considers its completion a cornerstone in the development of the region as a new 'Red Sea Riviera'.

THINGS TO SEE & DO
Pharaoh's Island ★★

The delightful getaway known as Pharaoh's Island is 7 km (4 miles) before the border and just 250 m (270 yd) off the coast. Dominated by the restored Castle of Salah ad-Din, it is a pleasant place to spend half a day enjoying some nice snorkelling and sunbathing. Return boat trips are available from the coast.

The fortress was built by the Crusaders in 1115, but captured and expanded by Saladin in 1170. At the height of the Crusades, it was considered a major defence post protecting the Muslim holy cities of Mecca and Medina. Some of the restoration jobs have been a bit haphazard, however, especially the bits where concrete has been used to shore up crumbling walls.

If it's snorkelling you're after, then you should head to the southern end of the island where the coral is good, or to the north-eastern coast where the reefs are even better. The south is the best place for rest and relaxation as the only café serving cold drinks is located here – but they definitely charge high prices for the service.

CROSSING THE BOARDER

The border with Israel is open 24 hours a day, despite the ongoing Palestinian political issues. The only exceptions are Yom Kippur and Eid al-Adha. No traffic whatsoever passes between the two nations on these two important holy days.

It is also advisable to avoid attempting to cross into Israel after mid-morning on Friday or all day Saturday when transport and businesses in Israel shut down for Shabbat.

Leaving Egypt Departing Egypt is a relatively quick and painless process, unless you wind up behind a large tour group. An exit tax is payable by everyone leaving the country regardless of age or nationality. Israelis issue free three-month visas to all EU, US, Canadian, Australian and New Zealand citizens.

Travellers must walk a no man's land between the Egyptian and Israeli checkpoints. Once past the Israeli checkpoints, it is then possible to catch a shared taxi or a bus to Eilat.

Coming from Israel There is an exit tax payable to Israeli authorities and there is an entry tax payable to the Egyptian government which is required by all travellers leaving Israel. Visas can be obtained in Tel Aviv or same-day from the Eilat consulate.

If you are just planning to travel within the Sinai peninsula, consider purchasing a 14-day, Sinai-only visa which is issued free at the border. Once across the border you may be approached by taxi drivers who try and convince you that the walk to the bus stop that takes passengers on to the coast towns of Nuweiba and Sharm is too far to walk. Do not listen to them. Even if you have a lot of luggage, it's really just a five-minute stroll away.

If you need Egyptian pounds, wait until you get into Egypt as the exchange rate in Israel is less advantageous.

From Hurghada

Mons Porphyritis ★

Located 40 km (25 miles) into the desert on a side track off the main coast road 20 km (12 miles) north of Hurghada is an ancient porphyry quarry known as Mons Porphyritis. Originally worked by the Romans, the mine produces a precious white-and-purple crystalline stone that was mined for use in sarcophagi, columns and decorative work. Much valued by Rome's imperial family, the mines had encampments, workshops and temples built specifically for the workers and engineers.

In order to transport the stone from the mine, blocks were dragged 150 km (93 miles) to the Nile, where they were then shipped to such locales as Baalbek and Constantinople. Lying around the quarries is a ruined town with two large cisterns and an unfinished Ionic temple. To get the most out of the visit, a guide is recommended. A large number of tours from Hurghada visit the area, making the town seem extremely crowded at certain times of the day – try and go off-peak (late afternoon).

St Anthony's Monastery

Mons Claudianus ★

Less historically important and more remote is Mons Claudianus. Also a Roman mining centre, Mons Claudianus was known for its output of black-flecked granite. Some of the stone produced here was used to construct the Parthenon and Trajan's Forum in Rome.

Only the most hardened of Roman prisoners were shipped to this desolate spot to work as forced labour, as it was considered to be an 'end of the line' destination. Guards fared little better – a spell here was considered a hardship post for soldiers of ill repute. The remains of the tiny cells they inhabited still exist, in addition to an immense cracked pillar, left where it fell 2000 years ago. A guide is also required for this trip, which you can usually arrange through your hotel.

Zafarana ★ ★ ★

Far from Hurghada, yet well worth the trip is the town of Zafarana. Gateway to the monasteries of St Anthony and St Paul, the town is an important centre for Coptic Christians.

St Anthony is a fortified religious community hidden in the barren cliffs of the Eastern Desert. Built in the 4th century AD, the site is located at the foot of Gebel al-Galala al-Qibliya – a location specifically chosen in order to help guard it against almost constant attacks from Bedouins and Muslims from the 8th to the 15th century. At certain points in its bloody history, the monastery could only be entered using a large basket and wooden winch. Ask nicely and the current residents will show you how it works.

Zafarana is easy to reach using regular bus routes that ply the road between Suez and Hurghada. Budget for at least two days to undertake the return journey from Hurghada.

Church of St Anthony The oldest part of the monastery is the Church of St Anthony, built over St Anthony's tomb. It contains the largest collection of Coptic wall paintings in Egypt all newly restored after exten-sive renovation. There are currently over 60 monks and five novices at St Anthony's, dedicating their lives to poverty, chastity,

obedience and prayer. The monks have almost completed construction on a museum that will better showcase the monastery's collection of manuscripts and crosses.

Monastery of St Paul The monastery of St Paul has always been overshadowed by St Anthony. Its founder was only sixteen when he fled his hometown of Alexandria in order to escape the persecution of Emperor Decius. Following his death, St Paul's followers decided to build a monastery to honour him. Much smaller than St Anthony's, the complex is more primitive looking than its better-known neighbour. Monks will show you around the chapels and identify icons.

From Marsa Alam

Rock inscriptions & ancient mines ★

A plethora of rock inscriptions exist on the Marsa Alam–Edfu road, many dating back to prehistoric times. Hunting scenes with dogs chasing ostriches, giraffe depictions and hieroglyphs are just some of the drawings that can be spotted. You don't have to travel far outside city limits to see drawings because the smooth grey rock of the area was perfect for carving. Police are nervous about foreigners travelling on roads, so a guide is recommended as much for your protection as to avoid police harassment.

Further afield are a number of ancient gold mines in the mountains south of town. Of particular interest is Wadi Miya, known for the remains of a temple said to be built by Seti I.

Among the other sites worth considering are **Wadi Hammamat**, **Wadi Mineh** and **Wadi Barramiyah**. Wadi Hammamat is celebrated for its beautiful hieroglyphs, Wadi Mineh for its wealth of petroglyphs and Wadi Barramiyah for its rock-cut Temple of Kanais. One of the best parts of any excursion into the desert is the actual drive. The landscape is wonderful and the road is almost empty except for the occasional grazing camel. Visitors can only reach these remote mines by foot or on camel with an experienced guide. Again, the police are extremely nervous about foreigners taking this road. Buses do run along the route, making drops at Wadi Hammamat from the coast road, but it is much easier to plan a visit as part of an organized tour. Another option is to hire a taxi for the day. Hiring a car and driver should be reasonably inexpensive.

For climatic reasons, trips to see the mines and inscriptions are recommended only from mid-September to mid-May. When setting out, ensure that you have enough water and fuel for your entire journey.

El-Quesir ★★

El-Quesir is a major port located almost exactly halfway between Marsa Alam and Hurghada. The town has a long history dating back to Pharaonic times, when it was a major launching point for boats sailing to Punt. The ancient port is now silted up, yet the modern town is still interesting.

El-Quesir is a particularly pleasant town to wander through due to its sleepy charm and intriguing architecture. Old coral-block buildings

● *Deserts are by no means all sand: take your chance to experience wilderness*

with wooden balconies surround the waterfront interspersed by the domed tombs of saints – there were mostly pious pilgrims who died en route to or from Mecca. Relax by pulling up a chair at the coffeehouse on the harbour to sip a Turkish coffee and watch the world go by.

Until the 10th century, El-Quesir was a major exit point for pilgrims travelling to Mecca for the haj. While its importance dwindled over time, the town remained strategically key and was fortified by the Ottomans six centuries later. The British took over the town in the 19th century, beating the French for control. At one point, it was the point of importation for all spices going to Britain from India. The opening of the Suez Canal in 1869 ended this period of prosperity, prompting a long period of decline.

The fortress The formidable fortress dominates the town, despite scars that remain from a heated battle between the British and occupying French forces in the 19th century when over 6000 cannonballs rained down on the structure.

Restoration work on the fortress was completed about two years ago, during which time a visitors' centre was built in order to display collections discussing local history, Red Sea mining, local monasteries, important trade in the region and the history of the haj.

Across from the fortress is the 19th-century shrine of a Yemeni sheikh. His gravestone is located in a niche in the wall of the building.

From Sinai resorts

Coloured Canyon ★★
Second only to St Catherine's as a day-trip destination, the Coloured Canyon derives its name from the layers of bright, multicoloured stones that resemble paintings on its steep, narrow walls. As the canyon is sheltered from the wind, it is extremely silent – a fact that contributes to its eerie atmosphere. Unfortunately, the sheer volume of visitors often means that you can't appreciate the calm as much as you might wish to.

The shades of colour that can be seen here range from white to yellow to vibrant red. They are particularly reminiscent of similar formations found at Petra in Jordan. Hikers will find that the colours are extremely well set off by the tiny strip of vivid blue sky above. At some points, the canyon can be just 1.5 m (5 ft) wide.

Coloured Canyon

A BRIEF HISTORY

Water erosion during the Quarternary Period provided the foundations on which the canyon developed. A glance at the spectacular landscape of the region will take you through eras of history, as you can see the many layers of sandstone, limestone and rocks of marine origin that have been carved by the erosion over thousands of years.

The narrowest and most impressive section of the canyon is about 700 m (765 yd) in length, and presents two passages that require considerable fitness to get through. After making your way through the section, you will find that the canyon widens a bit and enters a broad wadi. Keep to the right until you reach a rock cliff with a steep trail that will need to be climbed to return to the highland.

If you arrived here with a private driver, this makes a good location to arrange a pick-up – otherwise, you'll have to walk all the way back along the 2.5 km (1.5 mile) trail.

Gebel Musa ★★

The climb up Gebel Musa (which translates as the mountain of Moses), believed to be the same as Mount Horub from the Bible, is an excursion not to be missed by any travellers who tour St Catherine's. The hike to the summit requires about three hours and can be made by two different routes, which both converge along the final part of the hike. Sikket Saydna Musa (The path of Moses) is believed to follow the route taken by Moses when he first climbed the mount. It consists of a long, steep stairway of approximately 3700 steps cut directly into the living rock by the monks.

Spring of Moses After about 30 minutes, walkers pass this spring, which gurgles out into a small grotto and runs past a chapel dedicated to the Virgin Mary.

Gate of Confession After the spring and chapel, one encounters the Gate of Confession, so called because a monk once heard confession here from pilgrims in ancient times, in order that they might accede to the sacred mountain cleansed of their sins.

Amphitheatre Halfway up the mountain, walkers reach a plain surrounded by granite known as the 'Amphitheatre of the Seventy Wise Men of Israel' – called this because the Seventy Wise Men who accompanied Moses on his climb stopped here, because only the prophet could present himself in the presence of God.

Chapel of the Holy Trinity The summit of the mountain offers breathtaking views. There is also a chapel dedicated to the Holy Trinity that was rebuilt in 1934 on the grounds of an existing church from the 4th century AD. Its interior decoration illustrates the life of Moses using colourful frescoes. Alongside the chapel is a mosque that supposedly lies just above the cave where Moses spent 40 days and the Lord appeared to the prophet Elijah.

Nabq Mangrove Forest ★★

The region of Nabq , which extends over 600 sq km (200 sq miles) was declared to be a protected territory in 1992 and incorporated into the National Park of Ras Mohamed. The delicate natural equilibrium of this coastal strip justifies the policy of extremely strict environmental protection that is implemented by park authorities. The forest is a place of great beauty offering visitors the opportunity to observe a lagoon area teeming with life, in contrast with the silent void of the surrounding desert. The most numerous residents of the beaches are hermit and mud crabs. You'll see plenty of them scurrying on the sand.

Nabq holds the largest mangrove forest in the Sinai, extending along more than 4 km (2.5 miles) of the shoreline. These plants, with their distinctive roots on the water's surface filter sea water and expel salt crystals from the leaves. They also restrain sediments, thus limiting erosion on the entire coast line. A vast number of animal species call Nabq home.

Bird watchers will find the region of particular interest as numerous herons, ospreys and storks are drawn to the park in order to gorge themselves on the buffet of small fish that swim in the shallow waters surrounding the mangroves.

HOW TO GET TO NABQ BY CAR

Once past the Ras Nasrani airport, follow the paved road which runs parallel to the coast through a built-up area of hotels and tourist villages. After passing a small MFO military post, a short, narrow track leads to an old Egyptian military outpost where two cannon were installed during President Nasser's time to protect the Strait of Tiran. The road soon turns into a well-beaten track that passes a lighthouse until it reaches an Egyptian army checkpoint. When you reach the checkpoint, rangers will charge you to enter the park. ❶ Be sure to bring your passport or you will be turned back at this point.

Oasis of Ain Umm Ahmed ★★

Ain Umm Ahmed is one of the least visited and most beautiful oases in the Sinai. This is a huge palm grove broken here and there by small gardens and orchards cultivated by the few Bedouin families that live in a nearby village.

This is a place with abundant water, which springs forth pure and clear after travelling through long subterranean passages. It is gathered by the Bedouins in cisterns partially concealed amidst the palm trees.

A LUNAR LANDSCAPE

To best appreciate the oasis, look for a well-marked track near the Bedouin village that takes the same name as the oasis. It will climb to a narrow passageway between huge boulders that will then open up into a scenic point overlooking a broad expanse of powdery looking white rocks. Depending on how the light hits them, colours can leap up ranging from light blue to ochre and deep red. Especially worth noticing is the majestic Ras el-Qelb mountain that stands approximately 1000 metres (3300 feet) high. The track then becomes a true road that runs a number of metres wedged between the mountain and the deep multi-coloured sandstone bed of a dry stream.

BE PREPARED

Walkers particularly enjoy this stretch of protected land as there are a number of well-marked routes ideal for exploration. If you do decide to take a stroll, carry plenty of water and embark either early in the morning or in the late afternoon as the sun can get extremely hot. You must also stick to the pathways as the surrounding land is protected. A few steps off any trail could cause damage to an extremely fragile ecosystem. Please follow these simple rules: no camping, no fires, no smoking, no alcohol and no interfering with the wildlife and fauna.

Wadi el-Ain The sandy Wadi el-Ain is dotted with acacias, palm trees and wells that are protected by barbed wire. It is a stunning location for a spot of contemplation and the perfect ending point after a peaceful hike.

🛈 If you plan on visiting, be sure to bring your passport as there is a military checkpoint just before you reach the oasis. Without identification, the armed forces won't let you past their gates. Your journey will be much quicker if you have a driver and/or guide with you to handle the translation and act as your 'agent'.

Ras Mohamed ★★★

A national park since 1983, the peninsula of Ras Mohamed is located at the southern tip of the Sinai. It is an unspoilt site of remarkable beauty and exceptional interest in terms of nature and wildlife. The park has four goals that it strives to achieve:

- To provide information and education to visitors
- To explain the purposes of the park to the Bedouins, so that they can better manage their own land
- To promote scientific research and environmental monitoring
- To ensure that laws designed to protect the natural heritage of the park are adhered to.

🔺 *Ras Mohamed National Park*

Diving at Ras Mohamed Both the land and surrounding water are considered part of the park. As such, there are some incredible diving spots located just offshore. One of the best ways to arrive at the park is by sea as it allows visitors the opportunity to examine the magnificent seabeds. One of the best locations to see the interplay of both the land and marine ecosystems is from an observation platform called the 'Shark Observatory' on the east side of Hidden Bay.

St Catherine's Monastery ★ ★ ★

The monastery of St Catherine is located at the foot of the Gebel Musa, at an elevation of 1570 m (5150 ft) above sea level. Founded by the Byzantine emperor Justinian between AD 527 and 547, the complex boasts a fascinating history that can trace its roots back to the Bible.

According to the story of Moses, the tablets of the Ten Commandments were given to the Hebrews on the plain of El-Raha in the Sinai peninsula after 50 days of marching through the desert. Mount Horeb, which is located near the plain and has since been dubbed Gebel Musa (the Mountain of Moses) became a place of pilgrimage and prayer for the earliest Christians and a small monastic community was born.

While tours of the monastery are on offer, most of the buildings are off-limits to visitors. Rather, it is the surrounding countryside and grounds that make a visit here an absolute must. If you would like to

THE LEGEND
Between the 8th and 9th centuries, the monks found the body of St Catherine, which, according to legend, had been transported by angels to the summit of Gebel Katherina. The saint's body was placed in a sarcophagus inside the basilica where it still lies. It was the Crusaders of the 11th century who spread the cult of St Catherine throughout Europe, making the monastery one of the great Christian pilgrimage destinations.

include a tour in your itinerary, plan your visit in the morning hours as guides are only permitted between the hours of 9.00 and noon. Fridays, Sundays, major religious holidays and periods of spiritual retirement restrict access to the monastery. Check with your tour operator or hotel prior to setting off.

Tiran ★★

The island of Tiran is a diver's paradise. Enormously important in military terms, the island actually belongs to Saudi Arabia, yet is 'on loan' to Egypt. While you can't step foot on Tiran, the land mass is a wonderful location to visit as part of a day trip due to its enchanting diving opportunities.

Tiran is located at the centre of the strait of Tiran, which closes off the Gulf of Eilat and is bounded by the Sinai peninsula and the Saudi Arabian coast. The coral reefs off the south-eastern coast of Tiran and to the northwest are considered to be the best preserved in the entire Sharm region.

◆ *St Catherine's Monastery*

THE CORAL REEFS

Four coral reefs occupy the centre of the strait: Gordon Reef; Jackson Reef, and two smaller reefs, Thomas Reef and Woodhouse Reef. All are favourite diving spots for experienced divers, yet you will find few who talk about it, preferring to keep this jewel of a location as untouched as possible. Gordon Reef offers intriguing views thanks to the remains of a wrecked freighter that ran aground on the reef's coral shallows. Almost every species of coral fish can be found close to the freighter's slowly deteriorating shell.

ABUNDANT FAUNA

In these sites, the fauna is extremely abundant. Large fish and sharks are common due to the presence of powerful currents, which also promote the growth of alcyonarians and gogonians covering the walls of the reef. Divers and snorkellers have been challenged by these currents and are advised to always explore with a partner and/or experienced guide. Trips are easily arranged from Na'ama Bay.

◆ *A camel ride is an Egyptian experience not to be missed!*

Wadi Magara ★★

Fans of adventure will love taking an off-road trip to the Wadi Magara turquoise mines, which are reached by following an ancient track eastwards up Wadi Sidri from Abu Rudeis. The mines have been worked since as far back as the First Dynasty. As you walk deep into the valley, you may even notice small turquoises, though these are of little value. If you climb higher, you will come to carvings on the rock face depicting 4th- and 5th-Dynasty pharaohs. Directly across the valley, on the hill opposite, are the remains of workshops, workers' houses and a fort – all pharaonic.

King Sekhenkhet Back down on the sandy wadi floor, you can picnic beneath the shade of an acacia tree. Here, one can also see a celebrated bas-relief dating from the Old Kingdom, depicting King Sekhemkhet (Third Dynasty, about 2600 bc) that was uncovered by a British explorer in 1868.

Mines & inscriptions tour The Wadi Magara is best visited as part of a tour. Most packages to the mines will also include visits to the larger mines of Serabit el Khadim, where there is also a 12th-Dynasty sanctuary dedicated to the god Hathor. They will also stop at Wadi Moqattab, otherwise known as the Valley of the Inscriptions. Here you will find mostly Nabatean and Greek inscriptions, but also Coptic and Arabic texts dating from the 1st to 6th centuries ad.

Camel camping One of the most enjoyable ways to enjoy this region is to travel through it on camel. Camels with guides can be hired to venture to the Wadi from Dahab, Nuweiba, Sharm el Sheikh and St Catherine's. Treks will usually take from one to ten days.
❶ Be prepared to produce a medical certificate, and bring along your own sleeping bag and first aid kit. You may also be required to register your trip with the police for security purposes.

Alexandria & Aswan

ALEXANDRIA

In Cleopatra's day, Alexandria was a glittering jewel of a city. Sadly, little remains of its glorious past, however. Until recently, few had reason to visit Egypt's most European of cities, but recent innovations have changed all of that as numerous efforts are being made to transform the fortunes of this once proud metropolis. It is now a city that makes an interesting destination to combine with a visit to Aswan.

Biblioteca Alexandrina ★

This massive structure is Alexandria's most visible attempt to put the city back on the world's cultural map. Inspired by the original great library – one of the Seven Wonders of the Ancient World – the Biblioteca is designed to hold eight million books in its vast space. Unfortunately, the library's budget has fallen short of expectations and only a few hundred thousand works call the Biblioteca home. The most interesting aspect of the museum is a fascinating exhibit chronicling the history of the city through the use of drawings, maps and early photographs.

Catacombs of Kom Ash-Shuqqafa ★★

Home to the largest Roman burial site in Egypt, the catacombs were discovered accidentally in 1900 when a donkey fell through the ground. They are made up by three tiers of tombs and chambers cut into the rock to a depth of 35 m (115 ft). Entry into the catacombs is done by descending a spiral staircase cut into a circular shaft. If you are nervous about tight, dark or enclosed spaces, you may want to give this sight a miss.

Graeco-Roman Museum ★★

This excellent museum holds over 40,000 relics dating from as far back as the 3rd century BC. A recent renovation, completed in 2005, has restored the museum back to its former glory. Some of the more impressive exhibits include carved heads of the city's founder, Alexander and carvings of a part Egyptian, part Greek god by the name of Serapis.

◑ *Local produce at the market*

ASWAN

Egypt's southernmost city is the gateway to Africa and home to the bulk of the country's Nubian population. It's a prosperous marketplace at the crossroads of ancient caravan roads and is slowly becoming a popular resort town. The city is most often combined as a two-centre package with holidays in Marsa Alam.

Abu Simbel ★ ★ ★

Located 280 km south of Aswan, Abu Simbel is one of Egypt's 'signature' sights and is most often visited as a day excursion using regular charter flights. Two temples stare out from the cliff face at Abu Simbel – built by Ramses II as a warning against troublesome Nubians. Before the creation of Lake Nasser, the temples overlooked a bend in the Nile River and dominated the landscape. They remain as impressive as ever and are well worth the financial investment required to visit.

Construction of the Aswan High Dam in the 1960s would have drowned the temples beneath Lake Nasser. Instead, a massive operation funded by UNESCO raised them to a new and higher site nearby.

◐ *The Sphinx*

Kom Ombo ★★

The double Temple of Sobek and Horus, dating from the Ptolemaic period, enjoys a lovely setting on a low promontory overlooking the Nile. It's a bit of a long journey outside Aswan, often done in an overnight trip. One of the most enjoyable ways to arrive is to hire a felucca from Aswan and sail up the river, tying up beneath the temple to spend the night.

Philae ★★

The temple of Philae was moved to its present site, the island of Agilqiyyah, in 1980 following flooding caused by the completion of the Aswan Dam. Built over 2000 years ago in honour of the goddess Isis, the complex boasts a collection of minor temples in addition to three prin-ciple monuments: the Kiosk of Trajan, Temple of Hathor and Temple of Isis. It's an intensely romantic spot, especially at sunset.

Cairo & Luxor

CAIRO

Home to over 16 million inhabitants, Cairo is a teeming mass of humanity that seduces many a traveller with its chaotic corners, exotic alleyways and fascinating history. It's an easy city to combine in a two-centre package with Luxor.

Egyptian Museum ★★★

More than 120,000 relics and antiquities from every period of ancient Egyptian history are housed in the Egyptian Museum. The collection was first gathered under one roof by the French archaeologist Auguste Mariette in 1858 and transferred to its current location in 1902. The museum is now too small to house everything effectively and is literally bursting at the seams. Exhibits are arranged chronologically from the Old Kingdom to the Roman Empire, with the most popular room being the Tutankhamun Gallery. Try to arrange your visit first thing in the morning to avoid the huge crowds that descend on the building each day.

Khan al-Khalili ★★

Cairo's fascinating *souq*, located in the heart of the Islamic quarter of the city, has existed since the 14th century. Today, the Khan is a huge conglomeration of shops selling everything under the sun – even magic spells! A great way to pass the time is to enjoy a *sheesha* (pipe) and a Turkish coffee at Fishawi's Coffeehouse, which has been open continuously for the past 200 years in the centre of all the action.

Pyramids of Giza ★★★

One of the Seven Wonders of the World, the Pyramids of Giza represent Egypt like no other sight in the country. Built by three successive Pharaohs, they were already more than 2500 years old by the time of the birth of Jesus Christ. Please remember that a photography ticket is required if you plan to take pictures. The complex is open 8.00–16.00 every day, extended to 17.00 during the summer months.

LUXOR

Often combined as part of a two-centre holiday with Hurghada, Luxor (then known as Thebes) was the glittering capital of the Egyptian kingdom during the 18th and 19th dynasties. At the height of its glory, it had a population as high as one million. Packed with historical interest, Luxor is a convenient gateway for both the Red Sea coast and Nile cruises.

Temple of Karnak ★ ★ ★

The Karnak site covers a huge area. Dedicated to the god Amun, the complex is actually composed of several temples, with most visitors focussing their attentions on the massive, central place of worship – the Temple of Amun.

The temple complex is incredibly large due to the fact that each dynasty added to the site from its founding during the Middle Kingdom to the 25th dynasty, 1300 years later. Sound and light shows are held daily, but they are best avoided as they are packed with cliché after cliché and cheesy special effects.

Valley of the Kings ★ ★ ★

The Valley of the Kings is an oven of white sand containing 62 tombs, almost all belonging to pharaohs of the 18th, 19th and 20th Dynasties (1570–1090 BC). The tombs were cut into the soft limestone by workmen living in nearby Deir el Medina. Construction and decoration began as soon as a pharaoh came to the throne, and followed a similar pattern in all the tombs.

Three corridors lead to an antechamber connecting to a main hall with a sunken floor for receiving the sarcophagus. For fans of King Tutankhamun, it is here where his tomb was famously discovered by Howard Carter in 1922.

Excavations and restoration is constant in the valley. As such, tombs are open on a rotating schedule. Check in advance with your tour guide or hotel to confirm that the tomb you want to see will be open on the day.

◗ *Temple of Karnak*

Nile Cruise

A cruise is the perfect way to see the wonders of the River Nile and to explore the many ancient monuments and fascinating sights along the way. Although some boats cruise from Cairo to Aswan, most travel between Luxor and Aswan, and last three to five days.

THE CRUISE
Abydos ★★
Ancient Abydos was the shrine of Osiris, the god of the underworld. Osiris was a central figure in the Egyptian's notion of resurrection and the afterlife. The 19th-Dynasty New Kingdom pharaoh Seti I, built the complex at Abydos as part of a drive to reinstate a sense of Egyptian style popularised during the Old Kingdom.

Dendera ★
Buses will meet your boat to take you to the Ptolemaic Temple of Hathor at Dendera. The complex is reached via a 1 km (0.6 miles) walk along a peaceful country road. Try and go early in the morning when the area is surprisingly cool and fresh.

Edfu ★★
The present town of Edfu, on the west bank of the Nile, is spread upon the mound of the ancient city of Djeba. Here, according to myth, Horus avenged the murder of his father Osiris by defeating Seth in titanic combat. To mark this triumph of good over evil, a succession of shrines was built here from earliest dynastic times, culminating in the Ptolemaic Temple of Horus on the west side of town.

Esna ★★
Like other towns along the Nile, Esna was, until the end of the 19th century, a port of call for camel caravans crossing the desert from the Sudan. The focal point of the town is the Temple of Khnum, which is still in the process of being excavated.

Food & drink

LOCAL FOOD

The cuisine of Egypt is drawn from across the Middle East. Very few dishes can claim to be unique to the country – not a surprise considering the country's history of occupation by foreign empires and geographic location.

Approximately half of the dishes found in Egyptian kitchens have roots in Turkey, with Lebanon accounting for much of the rest. There are a few exceptions. Coptic Christians claim to have 'invented' *fuul*, *ta'amiyah* and *molokhiyya*, the making of which is said to be depicted in Pharaonic tomb paintings.

Egyptian cuisine is the food of the people – basic, filling and cheap. While it isn't fashionable, it is tasty and worth exploring.

STAPLES

Fuul and *ta'amiyya* are the most common form of fast-food found throughout the country. *Fuul* is made from small, brown beans soaked overnight, boiled, then mashed. The result is a paste that is drizzled with olive oil, lemon juice, salt, pepper and cumin. *Ta'amiyya* consists of mashed broad beans and spices fried in a patty, stuffed in a pitta and served with *tahini* and salad. Travellers may know it better as falafel. Pickled vegetables and slices of pitta are usually served with both dishes free of charge.

Most establishments dishing up *fuul* and *ta'amiyya* also serve *shawarma* (the Egyptian version of the doner kebab) and *kushari*.

MEZZE

Mezze, a tradition of dining on lots of small dishes and found primarily in Lebanese cuisine, isn't as popular in Egypt as it is in other Middle Eastern nations. There are, however, plenty of tasty Egyptian 'side orders' that would be considered part of a traditional mezze platter.

Mahshi consists of various vegetables, such as vine leaves or aubergines, stuffed with mincemeat, rice, onions, parsley and herbs.

Once stuffed, the vegetable is baked and served piping hot. Another tasty option is *babaghanoug* – similar to *hummus*, yet made from grilled aubergines.

If you are willing to broaden your tastebud's horizons, you may want to nibble on some offal. *Kibda firekh* (chicken livers) are much loved by locals. You'll know if you've been served a good example if they taste and look like paté. *Mokh* (brains) are also often dished up, yet are rarely sampled by Western travellers. They are served crumbled and deep-fried, garnished with salad.

For those with truly iron-clad stomachs, lamb's testicles are considered a delicacy and are usually served as part of a mixed grill.

MAIN DISHES

The two most popular main courses in Egypt are *kofta* and *kebab*. *Kofta* draws its roots from Turkey. It is mincemeat, usually shaped into a ball, flavoured with spices and grilled. *Kebab* is skewered and grilled chunks of meat – usually lamb. Chicken is also sometimes available. The meat is served on a bed of parsley with tomatoes and onions. Bread, *tahini* and salad are usually added on the side.

Other main options include *firekh* (chicken roasted on a spit) ordered by the half or quarter. For a picnic lunch, takeaway spit-roasted chickens are available from many eateries for between E£8 and E£12, depending on weight.

Hamam (pigeon) is a common delicacy, served stuffed with spices and rice. It can also be dished up in a stew, known as *tagen*, which is cooked in a deep clay pot with onions, cracked wheat, rice and tomatoes.

In the Sinai and Red Sea resorts, fish is commonly available, usually grilled simply and served with salad or chips. Try it baked in rock salt for a flavourful experience.

DESSERTS & SWEETS

Desserts in Egypt are invariably sweet and overwhelmingly sticky. Give an Egyptian something that would send most average folk into diabetic shock and they'll devour it with glee.

Baklava, a pastry made from wafer-thin layers of filo filled with crushed nuts, pistachios and covered in honey or syrup is the most common treat. *Kunafa*, is another option made by sieving liquid batter onto a sizzling metal sheet so that it sets in vermicelli-like strands, which are quickly removed so that the dough remains soft.

🔺 *Baklava*

Soft, sweet cheese or cream is then piled on top. This dessert is most commonly associated with Ramadan.

If you aren't a fan of pastry, don't fret! *Muhalabiyya* is a thickened milk cream often flavoured with rose water and sprinkled with chopped nuts or coconut. *Umm Ali* combines the taste sensations of thickened milk cream with sweetened pastry layers for the ultimate sticky treat.

DRINKS

Shai (tea) and *ahwa* (coffee) are commonly drunk by almost everyone. When ordering tea, make sure to tell your waiter to serve it with either no sugar (*min ghayr sukar*) or a little sugar (*sukar shwaiyya*) otherwise it will come heaped with sweetness. An even more refreshing possibility is to drink your tea with mint leaves. This is only offered in season. Ask for *shai na'na'*.

Coffee drinkers should always specify that they want filtered coffee when placing an order. To not do so will result in the presentation of thick, Turkish coffee. Seasoned drinkers love the stuff, others find it strong and gritty. Resembling espresso in consistency and size, it is an extremely powerful concoction and comes in various levels of sweetness. Unless you have tried it before, you should try it served 'medium sweet'.

Beware – do not drink the entire cup as the bottom third contains the coffee grounds!

In hotter months, hot drinks are often shunned in favour of more refreshing tipples. *Karkadai* is an iced beverage made from boiled hibiscus leaves and either lemon juice or yogurt. You'll recognize it by its distinctive, bright red colour.

In winter, warm your toes with *yansoon*, an aniseed drink preferred by Egyptian mothers for its reputed medical benefits, or *sahlab*, a warm drink made from semolina powder, chopped nuts and milk.

BEER & WINE

As Egypt is a Muslim nation, alcohol selection can be limited – especially during Ramadan. 'Stella' is the most common beer drunk by the Egyptian population, but not the Stella that you may be familiar with. Stella has been brewed in Egypt for over a century. Batches vary in terms of quality, so one bottle may taste completely different from the next. A light brew known as Stella Meister and a heavier option in the form of Stella Premium are available. Most stick with the basic brand. Try to have it served as cold as possible to get the best taste. If you are staying in El Gouna, you may also find yourself offered the locally produced Saqqara.

Egyptian wine comes in three varieties, none of which are considered particularly good. Choose from Cru des Ptolémées (white), Omar Khayyam (red) and Rubis d'Egypte (rosé).

VEGETARIANS

If you are vegetarian, you won't find it particularly difficult sticking to it – but you might be bored. The staple foods of *fuul* and *ta'amiyya* are perfect for your palate, as well as such mezze dishes as *hummus*, *tahini* and *babaghanoug*. After that, the list of options dies fast.

Egyptians find it difficult to understand the concept of vegetarianism. In order to get your point across, say *ana nabaatee* (if you are male) or *ana nabateeyya* (if you are female) to your waiter. Be warned: any dish that says it is vegetarian may be dubbed that because it consists mainly of vegetables, but it may also have chunks of meat, so ask first.

Menu decoder

Here are some of the authentically Egyptian dishes that you might encounter in local eateries and restaurants.

asabeeh Rolled filo pastry filled with pistachio, honey, pine and cashew nuts

babaghanoug Paste of aubergines mashed with tahina

balila Milk dish with nuts, raisins and wheat

baklava Flaky filo pastry filled with honey and nuts

barazak Flat, circular cookies sprinkled with sesame seeds

basbousa Pastry of semolina, honey and nuts

börek Triangles of light pastry stuffed with salty white cheese, spinach or mincemeat

fasoolyeh Green-bean stew

fatir A dish, similar to a pancake or pizza made of layers of filo pastry with sweet or savoury fillings

fattoush Salad of toasted bread, tomatoes, onions and mint leaves

firakh Chicken grilled or stewed and served with vegetables

fuul Broad (fava) beans served with oil and lemon, sometimes also with onions, meat, eggs or tomato sauce

hamam Pigeon, usually baked or grilled and served stuffed with rice and spices

hummus Chickpea paste mixed with *tahini*, garlic and lemon, sometimes served with pine nuts and/or meat. Hummus is actually the Arabic for 'chickpea' and is more commonly used to refer to this in Egypt

isfinjiyya Coconut slice

kebab Chunks of lamb grilled with onions and tomatoes

kibbeh Minced lamb, bulgur wheat and pine nuts shaped into a patty and deep-fried

kibbeh nayeh Ground lamb and cracked wheat served raw like steak tartare

kibda Chicken liver sautéed in lemon or garlic

kofta Mincemeat flavoured with spices and onions, grilled on a skewer

kunafa Vermicelli-like strands of cooked batter over a creamy sweet cheese base baked in syrup

kushari Mixture of noodles, lentils and rice topped with fried onions and a spicy tomato sauce

labneh A cheesy yogurt paste, which is often heavily flavoured with garlic or mint

loubieh French bean salad with tomatoes, onions and garlic

mahallabiyya Sweet rice or cornflour pudding, topped with pistachios

mahshi A variety of vegetables (peppers, tomatoes, aubergines, courgettes) filled with mincemeat, rice, herbs and pine nuts

makarona Macaroni 'cake' basked in a white sauce or mincemeat gravy

molukhiyya Jew's mallow, a leafy vegetable stewed with meat or chicken broth and garlic to make a dish that resembles slimy spinach

mushabbak Lace-shaped pastry drenched in syrup

muttabel Similar to *babaghanoug*, but the blended aubergine is mixed with *tahini*, yogurt and olive oil to achieve a creamier consistency

samak mashwi Grilled fish served with salad, bread and chips

shakshouka Chopped meat and tomato sauce, cooked with an egg on top

shanklish Salad of small pieces of crumbled, tangy, strong cheese mixed with chopped onion and tomato

shawarma Slivers of pressed, spit-roasted lamb, served in pitta bread

ta'amiya Balls of deep-fried mashed chickpeas and spices

tabbouleh Salad of bulgur wheat, parsley, sesame seeds, tomato, lemon and garlic

tahina Sesame seed paste mixed with spices, garlic and lemon, eaten with pitta bread

umm Ali Corn cake soaked in milk, sugar, raisins, coconut and cinnamon, served hot

wara einab Vine leaves filled with spiced mincemeat and flavoured with lemon juice

zalabiyya Pastries dipped in rose water

Shopping

ALABASTER
Vases, statuettes and ashtrays are often carved from alabaster. All too often you will be pestered by touts offering alabaster 'antiquities'. Most are two a penny, so if you like what you see then make an offer of approximately one tenth of the asking price.

ANTIQUITIES
Any antiquity you are offered is bound to be fake. There are some pharaonic, Coptic and Islamic artefacts available on the market, but they will be much more expensive than anything found on the street. It is illegal to export genuine antiquities without government approval.

BOOKS & PRINTS
Books on Egypt and Egyptology are a wonderful souvenir, as well as reproduced prints of Egypt-inspired painters such as the 19th-century Scottish artist, David Roberts.

BRASS & COPPER
Candlesticks, lamps, mugs and pitchers made from brass are beautiful and functional. If the item is something that you might eat off of or drink out of, make sure it is coated with another metal (such as silver) as brass and copper can be highly poisonous when combined with some substances.

CLOTHING & FABRICS
The *galabiyya*, a full-length traditional garment worn by Egyptian men is a popular piece of casual wear for both men and women.

GLASS
Muski glass, usually turquoise or dark brown and recognizable by its numerous air bubbles, has been handblown in Egypt for centuries. It is now turned out as ashtrays, candlesticks and glasses.

JEWELLERY

Egyptian jewellery mostly mimics the more obvious pharaonic motifs such as the *scarab* (good luck), *cartouche*, *ankh* (symbol of life), and the Eye of Horus. Items of Islamic motifs also exist, but are usually confined to hands and eyes used for warding off evil.

Other items worth considering are strands of turquoise or Bedouin silverwork.

LEATHERWORK, SHOES & ACCESSORIES

Handbags, belts, suitcases and hassocks are common. Egyptian leather is, however, not of the finest quality.

MUSICAL INSTRUMENTS

Traditional musical instruments are an intriguing purchase, whether to look at or to play. Options include the *oud* (lute), *rabab* (viol), *nai* (flute), *kanoon* (dulcimer), *tabla* (drum), *mismare baladi* (oboe), and *duf* (tambourine).

NARGILEHS

Sometimes known as a 'hubbly-bubbly', a *nargileh* is a water-pipe traditionally used to smoke sweet apple tobacco. The best *nargilehs* will have glass rather than brass bodies for holding the water.

PAPYRUS

Sheets of papyrus with pharaonic scenes painted on them are often made from banana leaves. To determine if you are purchasing the 'real thing', there is an easy test. Real papyrus can withstand being crumpled up. Banana leaves will crack if you attempt to bend them.

🔺 *Hubbly-bubblies at Luxor market*

SCENTS & SPICES

Egypt has been one of the world's greatest centres for spice trading and perfume essences for thousands of years. Almost every *souq* will have a plethora of stalls selling an array of colourful powders and scents.

WEAVINGS, CARPETS, TENTS & TAPESTRIES

Egypt is not well-known for its carpets or weaving traditions. You can sometimes find decent rugs produced from neighbouring countries or Bedouin weavings.

WOODWORK & INLAY

Wooden trays, chess boards and boxes intricately inlaid with mother-of-pearl and coloured bits of wood are surprisingly affordable. If you have the dosh, you may even consider investing in a *Mashrabiyya* – a carved wooden screen found in many traditional homes.

Kids

Egyptians are extremely indulgent towards children – theirs and anyone else's. You will find that your children will be welcomed wherever you go, including mosques, archaeological sites, fine hotels and restaurants.

You will need to be extra careful when watching your child. Many open excavations have no warning tape around it and traffic lights are non-existent, making street crossings perilous.

The unrelenting sun can cause havoc on a child's skin. Always make sure your child is carefully protected by a high-factor sunscreen and that it is reapplied each time they come out of the water. Long-sleeve clothing, hats and sunglasses are also highly recommended.

If you want some time alone, better hotels will usually provide child-minders, and private medical services are good if you need to see a doctor.

Children may well take more readily to the strangeness of the environment than you do, and they will probably find the scent and the bustle of a bazaar more interesting than a museum. Carriage or camel rides and sailing excursions are particular favourites.

TOP ACTIVITIES
Aquariums ★★
Hurghada has a small and very poorly funded aquarium that is worth a visit if your child wants to see 'Nemo' but is either too young or lacks the swimming skills needed to snorkel or dive. ❸ Corniche, Ad-Dahar. Admission is E£5. ❶ Be warned – the tanks are very small and some of the fish are not in the best of health.

Aquascopes ★★
Looking like something from a watery Bond film, the Aquascope is a futuristic version of a glass-bottom boat ride. It is a floating structure with a bubble-shaped cabin that is submerged underwater. Ten people

❰ *Scents and spices can be found in almost every souq*

at a time can enjoy the underwater world that is revealed below. The admission fee purchases one hour of enjoyment and bookings can be made at the Hor Palace hotel, just north of the InterContinental on the resort strip.

More traditional glass-bottom boat rides can be arranged through almost every hotel in town.

Camel rides ★ ★ ★

Camel journey's led by Bedouin guides are very popular with kids. Many include Bedouin tea or dinner, which your child may not be so keen to try. Try to arrange your trip with Bedouin guides at the Pigeon House in order to ensure authenticity and secure a good price.

Submarine rides ★ ★ ★

Sindbad Submarine in Hurghada offers rides that are very popular with adventurous kids, allowing families to plumb the depths, yet remain dry. The submarines accommodate up to 46 people per ride and carry passengers down as low as 22 m (72 ft) below sea level. The trip lasts two hours, of which an hour is spent on a boat travelling to the site where the sea is moored from the Sindbad Beach Resort. Bookings can be made at any hotel in town.

> If it is a really scorching hot day, there are many things to do indoors, or in the evening, when the heat of the sun has gone. Also – try to ensure that children wear protective covering on their heads – and it's not a bad idea for grown-ups to do the same!

WATER SPORTS

When letting your child go off for a swim, it is best to keep your eye on them at all times. Public beaches do not have lifeguards of any sort, while private resort coverage can be sketchy. Tides can be powerful and may challenge even good swimmers.

Sports & activities

As could be expected, sports and activities in the Red Sea resorts revolve mainly around water. Sharm el-Sheikh is widely considered to be one of the world's finest diving centres, while Hurghada is well-known for its windsurfing.

TOP WATER ACTIVITIES
Deep-sea fishing ★
Day trips can be arranged in a number of resort towns. It is usually best to book two to three days in advance to avoid disappointment. The cost of a full-day excursion is about £E400 per boat including equipment. **Hurghada** Marine Sports Club ☎ 065 44 48 61

Desert adventures ★★★
Sharm el-Sheikh and Marsa Shagra, located approximately 10km (6 miles) north of Marsa Alam, are wonderful spots from which to join hikes, jeep and camel safaris into the desert. **Marsa Shagra** Red Sea Desert Adventures (☎ 0122 46 78 26) from October through March. **Sharm el-Sheikh** Canyon Safari (☎ 069 60 09 97); Desert Blues Safari (☎ 069 60 09 99).

Diving ★★★
The Red Sea resorts of Egypt became famous as holiday destinations primarily due to the excellent diving conditions of the region. To list all the diving centres of the Red Sea resort towns would take pages. A better option is to consult your tour rep and/or hotel concierge in order to determine who the best diving operators are in town. If in doubt, sit at any of the waterside cafes and strike up a conversation with a few of the expat divers in order to get advice.

Paragliding and water-skiing ★★
Paragliding and water-skiing are only available at a limited number of centres. Make sure to check the quality of the equipment and establish

the reputation of the operator before you decide to try it out. The Arabia Beach in Hurghada has a good reputation amongst those in the know.
 Check your insurance – it may not cover either sport unless you select an 'adventure sports' option.

Snorkelling ★★

Snorkelling is a great option for those who are wary of diving, yet still want to witness the incredible undersea life in the Red Sea. It is also much more affordable if you are on a tight budget.

Hurghada Prince Sea Trips at the Four Seasons 065 54 98 82
Sharm el-Sheikh Fanous Moto Safari 069 60 30 59; Sun 'n' Fun 069 60 16 23

Thrills & chills ★★

Go-kart racing, bungee rockets and trampolining are some of the more adventurous activities available in Sharm el-Sheikh. Bookings can be made via your concierge.

Windsurfing ★★

Powerful gusts make Hurghada a great choice if you are an avid windsurfer. Many resorts have watersport centres where you can rent boards and wetsuits. Some of the better centres include:

Happy Surf Three Corners 065 54 78 16
Happy Surf Sofitel 065 44 72 61
Habri/Friendly Surfing Centre Hurghada Beach Resort 065 44 37 10

PUBLIC BEACHES

Most public beaches are extremely untidy and will bring unwanted attention from a cross-section of the Egyptian population. Private beaches offer the best options. Many hotels and resorts open their beaches to outsiders for a fee. Don't think about trying to sneak past security as paying guests are always given distinctively coloured bathing mats to separate them from outsiders.

Festivals & events

Religious festivals bring out the best in the Egyptian population, transforming the streets into a riot of colour and excitement. Egyptians are more than happy to welcome you into the celebrations, where you will find an atmosphere of infectious hospitality and bonhomie.

MUSLIM HOLIDAYS & EVENTS
Muslims follow a lunar calendar, resulting in varying festival dates.

Ramadan
During this month of fasting, practised by all Muslims, nothing is permitted to pass the lips between sunrise and sunset. After dark, however, more food is consumed in Egypt during this month than at any other time of year. When the sun sets, families and friends gather and the evening takes on a carnival atmosphere – an excellent time to explore the streets.

Eid el Fitr
This three-day festival at the end of Ramadan is the biggest party of the year. Family members from abroad will often fly in to celebrate.

Eid el Adha (Quarban Bairam)
This feast celebrates Abraham's willingness to sacrifice Isaac. It occurs in the month when the *Haj* or annual Pilgrimage, takes place. If an Egyptian has the funds, they will purchase a sheep for the feast, slaughter it and distribute portions to celebrate the occasion.

Ras el Sana el Hegira
The Islamic New Year begins on the first day of the month of Moharram. Quranic and other religious texts are read at this time.

Muslim and Christian *moulids*
A *moulid* is a festival in honour of a holy man. It usually takes on the characteristics of a medieval fair with popular entertainments and a

souq. The only national *moulid* is the Moulid el Nabi in honour of the Prophet's birthday on the 12th day of Rabei el Awal. Most *moulids* are very local events celebrated by just a single town or village.

WHIRLING DERVISHES
Mevlana, the 13th-century Sufi master who founded his sect of Whirling Dervishes at Konya in Turkey, also has followers in Egypt. Often banned in other Muslim countries, whirling dervishes strive to achieve mystical union with God through ecstatic whirling.

NON-MUSLIM HOLIDAYS
New year's Day 1 January
Christmas 7 January – Coptic Christmas is a low-key holiday only celebrated by Coptics. Coptic businesses close for the day.
Easter March/April – The most important Coptic holiday. All other businesses remain open.
Sham el Nessim March/April – This national holiday, celebrated by Egyptians of all faiths, falls on the first Monday after Coptic Easter and is considered a 'salute to Spring', with picnics and family gatherings.
Sinai Liberation Day 25 April – Official national holiday celebrating Israel's return of Sinai in 1982.
May Day 1 May – Official national holiday.
Revolution Day 23 July – Official national holiday commemorating the date of the 1952 coup when the Free Officers seized power.
National Day 6 October – Official national holiday celebrating Egyptian successes during the 1973 war with Israel.

International fishing tournament
Held at Hurghada and attended by anglers from all over the world, this tournament, in February, is a must for fans of deep-sea fishing.

South Sinai camel festival
Hundreds of sellers come from across the Middle East to sell prize camels, but the real fun is watching the animals race to the finish line.

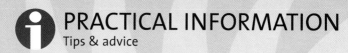

PRACTICAL INFORMATION
Tips & advice

Preparing to go

GETTING THERE

The cheapest way to get to Egypt's Red Sea Resorts is to book a package holiday with one of the leading tour operators. Tour operators specialising in Egypt offer flight-only, or combined flight-and-accommodation packages at prices that are hard to beat by booking direct. They can also arrange twin and three-centre holidays or packages that combine a Nile cruise.

BY AIR

Egypt has three international airports directly serving the Red Sea resorts (Hurghada, Marsa Alam and Sharm el-Sheikh) and two further major gateways (Cairo, Luxor) which are convenient if a twin-centre holiday is what you are after. All of the airports are not renowned for their efficiency and can become chaotic during peak season if there are delays. Numerous charter companies offer flights to the Red Sea resorts and Luxor throughout the year. Cairo is reserved exclusively for scheduled air traffic.

In the event that charter flights prove inconvenient, or you are looking to arrange a bespoke itinerary, the national flag carrier is EgyptAir. The airline flies throughout the country from its Cairo base and internationally throughout Europe, Africa, Asia and North America. Be warned: EgyptAir isn't renowned for being a particularly good airline when it comes to service. British charter flights are usually more enjoyable and better priced.

EGYPTIAN TOURIST AUTHORITY

Further information about Egypt can be obtained from the Egyptian Tourist Authority ❸ 170 Piccadilly, London W1V 9DD ❶ 0207 493 5283. Useful information can also be found on the Egyptian National Tourist Organization site (Ⓦ www.touregypt.net).

BEFORE YOU LEAVE

Holidays should be about fun and relaxation, so avoid last-minute panic and stress by making your preparations well in advance. It is not necessary to have inoculations to travel to Egypt, but you should make sure you and your family are up to date with the basics, such as tetanus and polio. If you are travelling beyond the Red Sea coast to locations in southern Egypt or sub-Saharan Africa, meningitis and typhoid vaccinations are a must.

It is always a good idea to pack a small first-aid kit to carry with you containing plasters, antiseptic cream, travel sickness pills, insect repellent, bite relief cream, antihistamine tablets, upset stomach remedies and painkillers. Women may also wish to pack feminine hygiene products as items available in Egypt will either be of poor quality or extremely expensive.

Sun lotion is more expensive in Egypt than it is in the UK, so it is worth taking a good selection of higher factor lotions in addition to after-sun cream.

If you are taking prescription medicines, ensure that you take enough for the duration of your visit – you may find it impossible to obtain the same medicines in Egypt. It is also worth having a dental check-up before you go as dentists in Egypt may not have the facilities or expertise to deal with problems.

DOCUMENTS & VISAS

The most important documents you will need are your tickets and your passport. Check well in advance that your passport is up to date and has a minimum of six months left to run. All children, including newborn babies, need their own passport unless they are already included on the passport of the person they are travelling with. It generally takes three weeks to process a passport renewal. This can be longer in the run up to the summer months. For the latest information on how to renew your passport and the processing times, call the Passport Agency on ❶ 0870 521 0410, or access their website Ⓦ www.ukpa.gov.uk.

You should check the details of your travel tickets well before your departure, ensuring that the timings and dates are correct.

If you are thinking of hiring a car while you are away, you will need to have your UK driving licence with you. If you want more than one driver for the car, the other drivers must also have their licences.

Visitors to Egypt require a visa to enter the country. Citizens of most countries, including the UK, Ireland the USA, Canada and Australia can obtain tourist visas on arrival in the country if landing at Cairo, Luxor or Hurghada airports. Visas obtained on arrival are valid for one month from the date of entry.

If you are planning a longer stay, or are arriving at Aswan, Suez or Nuweiba, you will have to get your visa from an Egyptian embassy or consulate. Visas obtained from an embassy are valid for three months and cost £15. The Egyptian embassy in the UK is located at ⓐ 2 Lowndes St, London SW1X 9ET ❶ 020 7235 9777.

MONEY

Egypt's unit of currency is the Egyptian pound, which is divided into 100 piastres. It is a good idea to have at least three days of survival money in cash with you upon arriving in the country. Don't worry if this proves impossible prior to departure as there are always numerous bank kiosks offering currency exchange services around the clock at every airport in the country. Traveller's cheques are the safest way to carry money as money will be refunded if the cheques are lost or stolen.

INSURANCE

Have you got sufficient cover for your holiday? Check that your policy covers you adequately for loss of possessions and valuables, for activities you might want to try – such as scuba-diving, horse-riding, or water-sports – and for emergency medical and dental treatment, including flights home if required.

CLIMATE

Average daytime temperatures in Red Sea resorts: January 21°C (70°F); March 23°C (74°F); May 30°C (86°F); July 32°C (90°F); September 30°C (86°F); November 25°C (77°F).

You will often find temperatures vary greatly over the course of the day and can reach as high as 50°C (120°F) in hot years. This is due to the dryness of the air and the absence of cloud.

BAGGAGE ALLOWANCE

Baggage allowances vary according to the airline, destination and the class of travel, but 20 kg (44 lb) per person is the norm for luggage that is carried in the hold. Charter airlines often have more limited restrictions, so it is best to check your ticket or contact the airline before departing.

You are also allowed one item of cabin baggage weighing no more than 5 kg (11 lb) and measuring 46 by 30 by 23 cm (18 by 12 by 9 inches). In addition, you can usually carry your duty-free purchases, umbrella, handbag, coat and camera as hand-baggage. Large items – surfboards, golf-clubs, collapsible wheelchairs and pushchairs – are usually charged as extras and it is a good idea to let the airline know in advance that you want to bring these.

During your stay

AIRPORTS

All Red Sea airports are served by paved roads, but if you are driving your-self, always allow plenty of time to reach the airport when flying back.

BEACHES

As a tourist, you will most likely use the stretch of beach owned by the prop-erty you are staying at. If your resort is not located directly on a beach, your other alternative is to purchase day entry at a resort that does. Public beaches are not recom-mended as they are often unclean and draw unwanted attention from locals and souvenir sellers.

⏺ *Resort beaches are best for lazy days in the sun*

Lifeguards usually aren't present except in five-star properties, so if you are travelling with children it is best to keep your eye on them at all times. Strong winds, especially around Hurghada, can change a safe beach into a not-so-safe one at a moment's notice. Currents can be tricky for even strong swimmers the further away from the coast you go. If in doubt, ask your local tour representative or at your hotel.

EMBASSIES

The British embassy is located at ❷ 7 Sharia Amerika Latina in Garden City, Cairo ❶ 027 94 08 52. Consulates or representatives can also be found in Luxor, Alexandria and Port Said, however, their powers are limited and they may direct you to the embassy in serious cases.

CURRENCY

Egypt's basic unit of currency is the Egyptian pound and it is written as either £E or LE. Banknotes are written in Arabic on one side and Western numerals on the other. Each bill is colour coded: £E1 (brown), £E5 (blue), £E10 (red), £E20 (green), £E50 (red), £E100 (green). You will almost never use the £E50 or £E100 notes as they are often forged and almost never accepted by shopkeepers. Always keep hold of as many small bills as possible as finding change for larger denominations can sometimes prove to be a challenge.

The Egyptian pound is divided into 100 piastres. There are 10pt, 25pt and 50pt notes and variously sized coins to the value of 5pt, 10pt, 20pt, 25pt and 50pt.

Egyptian banks are generally open Monday to Thursday 8:30–14.00, plus an evening shift of 17.00–20.00 in winter or 18.00–21.00 in summer. Some larger branches also open on Saturdays and from 10.00–noon on Sunday. Most foreign banks are open from 8:30–13.00 Monday to Thursday and Sundays.

Cash machines taking major bank cards are increasingly common in all the major resorts, however, power fluctuations and computer errors do happen and can result in having your card swallowed by the machine. Be smart and record your card number, emergency telephone numbers and inform the bank whose machine has your card as soon as possible to avoid and problems. A spare card is also a wise precaution that gives you access to additional emergency funds.

CUSTOMS

Egyptians are naturally an extremely friendly and welcoming people – as long as you follow a few simple rules. If you are a keen photographer and you wish to take the photograph of a person, you must ask their permission before doing so, especially in rural, remote communities where taking a photo can actually cause serious offence. Some locals may prevent you from taking a picture if it portrays Egypt in a bad light. You should also avoid taking any photos of military installations. If a soldier sees you doing so, then you could find yourself in seriously hot water.

Photographs are a great way to break the ice with locals. Be sure to bring a collection of family photos as they make great ice-breakers and exchanging them can lead to the development of a new-found friendship.

When entering a private home, it is common to remove your shoes as a sign of respect. It is also customary to take a gift. Sweet pastries or tea and sugar are always gladly accepted.

Always use your right hand for every public function such as passing a gift or holding a glass. In Egyptian culture, the left hand is used for 'unclean' things such as wiping your bottom and is considered unhygienic. While you can do things such as ripping a piece of bread off while holding the stick in your right hand, you should never actually place the food in your mouth or put it into a communal bowl with your left hand. Due to the heat, a midday siesta is common. Many shops and services will shut down for a few hours during the afternoon. If you are planning a full day of shopping or need to hit a bank, be sure to go in the morning.

DRESS CODES

Shorts are only acceptable to wear on a daily basis in the Red Sea beach resort towns – and only for men. Women should only wear shorts while relaxing in private resorts. Shirts for both sexes must always cover the shoulders. If you plan on visiting any cultural sites, women should wear skirts that go well below the knee and a shirt. A scarf to cover the hair is also recommended. Men should wear full-length trousers and a shirt.

ELECTRICITY

Voltage in Egypt is 220 volts which is compatible with the UK, but you will need a 2-pin adaptor to fit Egyptian sockets. It is important to realise that electricity is expensive in Egypt, so please be considerate in your use of it; for example, do not leave air-conditioning on in your room when you go out. There may be power cuts due to excessive demands on the local grid, but these rarely last long. Bring a flashlight with you to ensure safety. If you are considering buying electrical appliances to take home, check that they will work in the UK before you make your purchase.

FACILITIES FOR VISITORS WITH DISABILITIES

Egypt is sadly lacking in facilities for travellers with mobility problems. Ramps are non-existent, public buildings are difficult to enter and manoeuvre and kerbs are extremely high. Despite this, you will find that locals are keen to assist you if you get into difficulty.

GETTING AROUND

Driving rules and conditions In Egypt, you drive on the right. An international driving licence is an absolute must. If you are caught driving without one, you will be subjected to a heavy fine. The official speed limit is 90 km/h (56 mph) outside towns and 100 km/h (61 mph) on major highways – although this is often broken by locals. If you are caught speeding, your licence will be confiscated and you will have to go to the traffic headquarters in the area to get it back. This is a lengthy process that can ruin a holiday.

Many roads have checkpoints where police will ask for identity papers, so always have your passport available and driving licence on-hand or you may have to pay an on-the-spot fine.

Driving is chaotic across the country, however, there is one rule of the road that is commonly accepted by all. Whoever is in front has right of way – even if it is just by a single centimetre. If a car is a hair's breadth ahead of you and decides to cut across your path, you will be liable if you hit it. Children and adults tend to cross the road wherever they feel like it – even on major roads. Always keep your eyes peeled and use your horn often. If you hit someone, you could find yourself at the centre of an angry mob, whether or not you were at fault.

In order to do have an accident, get to the nearest police station as fast as possible to report the incident.

Car hire Most international car rental firms have offices in Egypt, including Avis, Budget, Europcar, Hertz and Thrifty. Rates are in line with international charges making a really cheap deal a rare find. No matter which firm you go with, be sure to read every inch of your agreement as terms and conditions can differ wildly. Most rental agreements include insurance and the first 100 km (61 miles) as part of the price package, but it is always wise to check before signing anything. Unlimited mileage options are also available, but should be avoided if you are plan-ning to stick firmly to your resort town as there is often a seven-day minimum. It is also important to note that any price quoted to you will not include a mandatory 10 per cent to 17 per cent tax added to your final bill.

In order to rent a car, drivers must be over the age of 25. Some companies, such as Europcar offer the option of a one-way rental from, for example, Sharm el-Sheikh to Cairo. It is also possible to hire a car and driver if you feel unsure about tackling Egyptian roads.

Public transport In the Red Sea resorts, service taxis are the cheapest option to use if you want to get around. Every town in Egypt has a service taxi station that has a collection of battered Peugeot's and even more battered drivers. To use one, find a driver who is going in your direction and get in.

Be warned: Service taxi journeys are not the most enjoyable method of transport as the driver won't depart until the entire vehicle is full. If you want a more comfortable trip, you can pay for additional seats to get the car moving. Service taxi drivers often work extraordinarily long hours, so do make sure you find one who looks wide awake to avoid any potential danger.

Taxis in Egypt are extremely cheap and easy to hail. Do be prepared for the driver to stop and take on other passengers. Always have the correct fare in small bills available as the driver will never have any change if they think they can get away with taking a large tip.

HEALTH MATTERS

Medical help Medical care is not always readily available outside major cities. Even some of the larger resort towns lack full-service facilities and may require you to be sent to Cairo in the event of a major accident or illness. Medicine, and even sterile dressings or intravenous fluids, may need to be bought from a pharmacy.

Pharmacies Egyptian pharmacies often have English-speaking staff and are very helpful for minor complaints and illnesses. They can provide valuable advice and sell over the counter medication and prescription drugs – often costing less than in England. Antibiotics, however, are usually much more expensive. Be warned: Pharmacies keep erratic hours and may not be open during the hot hours of the afternoon or on weekends (Fridays/Saturdays).

If you are prescribed drugs during your stay due to illness or accident, you should be able to reclaim the cost through your medical insurance. Pharmacies are not like chemist shops in the UK, so you are unlikely to find everything that you might need. You are advised to purchase condoms and feminine sanitary items prior to departure as the quality of these items in Egypt are far from Western standards.

Most major resorts do sell sunscreen, but you will find that the selection of high factor creams is limited and usually very pricy. Homeopathic and herbal remedies are not popular in Egypt, so it would be wise to stock up before arriving in the country.

Water Tap water is not safe to drink anywhere in Egypt. Always stick to bottled water, which is readily available throughout the country.

When purchasing your bottle, be sure the top has not been tampered with before drinking. Also check that any ice put in your drinks is made only from purified water.

Precautions Cooling breezes off the coast can mask the intensity of the sun's rays, which can burn you if deflected off the sand or nearby water. You can even burn in the shade, especially if you have sensitive skin. Keep covered up during the hottest part of the day and drink plenty of water to avoid dehydration.

In order to avoid snake bites, do not walk barefoot or stick your hand into holes or cracks. If bitten, immobilize the bitten limb with a splint and apply a bandage with firm pressure over the wound. Do not apply a tourniquet, cut or suck the bite. Seek medical attention as soon as possible in order to receive the necessary antivenom.

Mosquitoes can be a nuisance but are easily dealt with by burning insect coils or using an electric deterrent. Using a DEET-based insect repellent is also advisable to prevent bites. Malaria is not carried by mosquitoes in the Red Sea coastal areas, however, dengue fever is a remote possibility.

THE LANGUAGE
Arabic is the official language of Egypt, however, the dialect used in the country differs incredibly from Arabic spoken in other parts of the Middle East. While many of the root words are similar and 'educated' conversation remains understandable to Arabic speakers, the Egyptian 'street' dialect is often incomprehensible even to visitors from foreign Arabic-speaking lands.

There is no written form of the Egyptian Arabic dialect. If, however, you take the time to learn a few words and phrases, you will find that you can experience much more than the average tourist and will be greeted warmly by the Egyptian people.

Arabic is divided into masculine and feminine forms. Always use the correct form when addressing someone in conversation (see Useful Phrases, pages 120–121).

THE ARABIC ALPHABET

Arabic	Transliteration	Pronounced
ا	a/aa	as in father/as in can
ب	b	as in baby
ت	t	as in two
ث	th	as in three
ج	g	as in go
ح	H	a whispered 'h', almost like a sigh
خ	kh	as the 'ch' in the Scottish loch
د	d	as in do
ذ	dh	as the 'th' in this
ر	r	a rolled 'r', like the Spanish word pero
ز	z	as in zipper
س	s	as in so
ش	sh	as in shingle
ص	S	an emphatic 's'
ض	D	an emphatic 'd'
ط	T	an emphatic 't'
ظ	Z	an emphatic 'z'
ع		a glottal stop, like the closing of the throat
غ	gh	a guttural sound, similar to the French 'r'
ف	f	as in foul
ق	q	a strongly guttural 'k' sound
ك	k	as in king
ل	l	as in lemon
م	m	as in me
ن	n	as in now
ه	h	as in hair
و	w/oo/ow	as in woman/cool/how
ي	y/ee/ai/ay	as in yes/ear/aisle/may

Useful words and phrases	Arabic
Yes	*aiwa (or) na'am*
No	*la*

Useful words and phrases	**Arabic**
Please	*min fadlak (m)/fadlik (f)*
Thank you	*shukran*
Hello	*assalaamu aleikum (formal)/salam 'aleikum (informal)*
Goodbye	*ma'a salaama*
Good night	*tisbah (m)/tisbahi (f) 'ala kheer*
Excuse me	*an iznak (m)/'an iznik (f)*
Sorry	*aasif (m)/asfa (f)*
Help!	*el-Ha'nee!*
Today/tomorrow	*innaharda/bukkra*
Yesterday	*imbaarih*
Right/left	*yimeen/shimaal*
How much (is it)?	*bi-kam (da)?*
Where is a bank/post office?	*feyn il-bank?/al-boosta?*
Where is the bus station?	*feyn mahattat il-autobees?*
Doctor/hospital	*doktoor/mustashfa*
Police	*bolees*
I want...	*ayyiz (m)/ayyza (f) haga*
Menu	*lista/menoo*
Toilets	*al-twalet*
Mineral water	*mayya ma'adaniyya*
Bread	*'aish*
Salt/pepper	*melh/filfil*
Fish/meat	*samak/lahma*
Beer/wine	*beera/nibeet*
Turkish coffee	*'ahwa*
...very sweet	*ziyaada*
...medium sweet	*maazboot*
...no sugar	*saada*
Instant/filter coffee	*'ahwa fransawi*
The bill	*el-hisaab*
I don't understand	*ana mish fahem (m)/fahma (f)*
Do you speak English?	*Titkallim (m)/titkallimi ingleezi?*

MEDIA

If you don't speak Arabic, then your diet of news will be restricted to satellite television broadcasts. There is one very thin English daily newspaper, *The Egyptian Gazette* (also known as the *Egyptian Mail on Saturdays*), however, writing standards are very poor. *CNN* is usually found in almost all major resorts, with occasional American comedy and drama available on more extensive networks.

English newspapers are more difficult to find and are often long out of date by the time they reach newsstands.

OPENING HOURS

Traditional shopping hours in Egypt are 09.00–13.00 and 17.00–20.00 or later. In heavily touristed areas, some shops may remain open throughout the day. Some shops close on Fridays, while many more close on Mondays.

During the month of Ramadan, shop hours are severely reduced, with many establishments open only from 10.30–15.30 and 20.00–22.00 or later.

PERSONAL COMFORT & SAFETY

Crime You and your possessions are generally safe in Egypt. Nevertheless, take special care with passports, tickets, and money. Hotels will look after your valuables for you, but you should obtain a receipt. If the property has in-room safe facilities, use them. Don't flash expensive jewellery or merchandise around when you are walking and be sure to keep a close eye on your valuables when travelling on public transport as pick-pocketing can be a problem.

Police The police have a high profile in Egypt. In fact, Cairo has more police officers per capita than any other city in the world. There are many different police forces, each with a separate and distinct area of responsibility. Municipal police handle all crimes and keep law and order in smaller towns. Traffic police are in charge of motoring accidents and assist in emergencies. Tourist police are where you should report thefts and receive documents for insurance purposes. Central security forces guard embassies, banks and major government institutions, while state security patrol border areas and Middle Egypt.

Public toilets Apart from better hotels and restaurants, toilets will be of poor standard. Never count on there being toilet paper and, if there is, you will probably have to place used sheets in a bin. Egyptian plumbing cannot cope with flushed paper. Squirters are sometimes provided, or a bucket of water with which you are expected to splash yourself.

Restricted areas Avoid any bases and take heed of all signs near them. Failure to do so could result in your arrest. Never take any photographs of airports, highways, government buildings, or commercial ports.

POST OFFICES

Post between Egypt and foreign countries can be efficient as long as you use letter boxes at a major hotel or central post office. Some letter boxes are visited by postal employees only very rarely, if at all. Anything that isn't a simple letter or postcard can take ages. Post offices are open 08.30–15.00 daily, except Friday. If in doubt, purchase your stamps at your hotel and ask them to post articles on your behalf.

RELIGION

About 90 per cent of Egypt's population is Muslim. While Islam prevails in Egyptian culture, very few pray the specified five times a day. Friday noon is the exception, when almost every male in the country heeds the call to prayer. The remaining 10 per cent of the population is Coptic Christian. The two populations live in relatively peaceful co-existence.

If you ever wish to visit a mosque, always ask permission and make sure to remove your shoes before entering.

TELEPHONES

Local and international telephone services are available in most hotels. Local calls can also be made from some kiosks, shops, and restaurants.

International calls can be made from PTT offices. Normally you pay first for a fixed number of minutes. For assistance, dial 10.

If you are thinking of taking your mobile phone to Egypt, it is advisable to check first with your supplier to see if it will work.

TIME DIFFERENCES

Egypt is in the same time zone as Eastern Europe, so two hours ahead of the UK and one hour ahead of Central European time. Clocks go forward one hour on the last Friday in April and back one hour in October.

TIPPING

Tipping, otherwise known as *baksheesh*, is common practice in Egypt. A tip will be required (if not expected) to get anything done, no matter how small. The basic rule is to offer *baksheesh* only in return for a service, and not to pay until the service has been performed. Resist any forms of intimidation, especially from children who may pester you.

EMERGENCY NUMBERS
For an ambulance or help in an emergency call:
Ambulance ☎ 123
Police ☎ 122
Fire brigade ☎ 125

PHONING ABROAD
To call Egypt from the UK, dial 00 20 then the remaining seven- or eight-digit number (minus the initial zero).
To call overseas from Egypt, dial 00, then the country code (UK=44), then the area code (minus the initial 0) followed by the number.

ACKNOWLEDGEMENTS

We would like to thank all the photographers, picture libraries and organizations for the loan of the photographs reproduced in this book, to whom copyright in the photograph belongs:
Eddie Gerald/Alamy (Page 59); JupiterImages Corporation (Pages 96, 109, 125); Nick Hanna/Alamy (Page 46); Peter Raven/Mark Custance/Alamy (Page 80); Sarkis Images/Alamy (Page 75); Simo/Alamy (Page 44); Thomas Cook Tour Operations Ltd (pages 9, 11, 13, 16, 18, 28, 34, 39, 54, 62, 71, 77, 83, 84, 87, 91, 93, 101, 102, 113); World Religions Photo Library/Alamy (Page 72).

We would also like to thank the following for their contribution to this series:
John Woodcock (map and symbols artwork);
Becky Alexander, Patricia Baker, Sophie Bevan, Judith Chamberlain-Webber, Stephanie Evans, Nicky Gyopari, Krystyna Mayer, Robin Pridy (editorial support); Christine Engert, Suzie Johanson, Richard Lloyd, Richard Peters, Alistair Plumb, Jane Prior, Barbara Theisen, Ginny Zeal, Barbara Zuñiga (design support).

Send your thoughts to
books@thomascook.com

- **Found a beach bar, peaceful stretch of sand or must-see sight that we don't feature?**

- **Like to tip us off about any information that needs a little updating?**

- **Want to tell us what you love about this handy, little guidebook and more importantly how we can make it even handier?**

Then here's your chance to tell all! Send us ideas, discoveries and recommendations today and then look out for your valuable input in the next edition of this title. And, as an extra 'thank you' from Thomas Cook Publishing, you'll be automatically entered into our exciting monthly prize draw.

Email to the above address or write to:
HotSpots Project Editor, Thomas Cook Publishing, PO Box 227, Unit 15/16, Coningsby Road, Peterborough PE3 8SB, UK.